START **WRITING** YOUR BOOK TODAY:

A Step-by-Step Plan to Write Your **Nonfiction** Book, From First Draft to Finished Manuscript

MORGAN GIST MACDONALD

START WRITING YOUR BOOK TODAY:
A Step-by-Step Plan to Write Your Nonfiction Book, From First Draft to Finished Manuscript

"The most pernicious aspect of procrastination is that it can become a habit. We don't just put off our lives today; we put them off until our deathbed.

Never forget: This very moment, we can change our lives. There never was a moment, and never will be, when we are without the power to alter our destiny. This second, we can turn the tables on Resistance.

This second, we can sit down and do our work."

— Steven Pressfield, *The War of Art*

CONTENTS

Introduction I

Chapter One
What it really takes to be a successful author 5

Chapter Two
Preventing self-sabotage 17

Chapter Three
Good writing habits 24

Chapter Four
Writing the first draft 49

Chapter Five
Beyond the first draft 71

Chapter Six
Dealing with criticism 95

Chapter Seven
Finished manuscript 102

Gratitude 104

About the Author 106

Appendix A
Resources to help your book-writing journey 107

Appendix B
Tracking your progress 110

Appendix C
How to Create a Reverse Outline 114

Reverse Outline Sample Text
Excerpt from chapter "Good writing habits" 119

Reverse Outline Sample
Chapter: Good writing habits 126

Appendix D
Feedback Table 128

DEDICATION

To baby Meredith —
the happiest morning writing companion.

Introduction

You want to write a book. If you're honest, you've wanted to write a book for a *long* time, but when you sit down to start, the words get stuck. You feel your body tighten and frustration rise. The ideas are in there, floating in your mind, but here you are, unable to put words to those very ideas. So, back you go... to thinking, stewing, pondering, or any other euphemism you use for procrastination.

You wonder if maybe there's a trick to writing a book that you don't know. You read books from successful authors about how they write—Stephen King, Anne Lamott, Ernest Hemingway, Virginia Woolf, William Zinsser, Steven Pressfield. Surely, the next book on writing you pick up will impart the secret wisdom you've been missing all this time.

And then you pick up *this* book. Maybe it was the title that caught you, the promise of a roadmap from first draft to finished manuscript.

Maybe you resonate with the feeling that you want to start writing your book *today*, not next week, not next month. Maybe you're tired of putting off that life you want—the life of being a published author, whose books make a difference in people's lives. Let's talk about what this book, *Start Writing Your Book Today,* is and is not. And how it can propel you to start writing your own book.

You'll find *Start Writing Your Book Today* most useful if:

- You want to write a book, but you aren't clear about exactly what the book will be about. I'll provide exercises to give you clarity.
- You are a motivated, excited writer. You're done procrastinating, and this book's step-by-step plan is guaranteed to work, as long as you can bring the energy, from start to finish.
- You want to make a shift in your life and the lives of people around you. This book will show you how to harness the power of your words, so they can change the world.

In my years as a writing coach, I've come to realize that starting the first draft book often seems like it will be the hardest part, but it's not. Convincing yourself that your book is worth all the sacrifice of time, energy, money, and everything else in life—that's the hardest part of writing a book.

But let me promise you this: if you manage to keep in mind that your book is worthwhile, then you absolutely *can* write a book. Your grammar doesn't have to be perfect; your idea doesn't have to be worthy of a Nobel Prize; your life doesn't have to have room for four hours of writing a day. If you can hold on to the belief that your book will change your life and others', you can write a book.

In this book, I will coach you, just like I do with my author clients. I'll give you all of my best advice and walk you through what it looks like to write a book, how long you should plan to write every day, what writing a first draft feels like, how to go back and revise, how to solicit helpful feedback from editors and beta readers, and how to receive criticism in a way that strengthens your manuscript. I'll let you know where your greatest struggles will lie, and I'll encourage you through the process.

I'm going to be completely honest with you throughout this book. I believe, as you finish the last chapter of *Start Writing Your Book Today*, you'll feel competent, even compelled, to start writing your own book. As long as you don't stop there, you will finish it.

I'll be here, cheering you on the whole way. Even better, I'd love to get involved as you start your book. Hearing about you and the book you're about to write helps me help you more. I read every single email, and I would love to receive an email from you. Please to share with me what you're writing about by sending me an email at morgan@morgangistmacdonald.com.

CHAPTER ONE

What it really takes to be a successful author

It takes a lot of guts to call yourself a writer. Even more to mean it. At social gatherings, you dread being asked, "What do you do?" Maybe you throw in a quick "I write a little on the side," and hope the conversation changes quickly. That first time you work up the nerve to say, "I'm a writer," you feel a bit like a fraud. Why is that? Why do you have that sudden desire to dash away any true claims to the title? Why do you want to add a phrase to soften the boldness of the claim? "I'm sort of a writer, you know, when I have time," or "I'd like to be an author one day. I even have some ideas. I just haven't actually published anything yet."

There are many misconceptions about what it takes to be a successful author. I'm here to bust through those myths, to let you know that all of those assumptions you have about what authors are like or what kind of person you have to be are completely false. Then, we'll talk about what it *really* takes.

Myth: Authors have special, God-given, divinely inspired talents that enable them to put words and phrases together effortlessly.

Truth: Successful authors struggle with what words to use, how to describe a concept, and what to write about next—just as much as the rest of us. What distinguishes authors is *perseverance.* When authors aren't quite sure what words to use, they don't just throw up their hands in despair—they put down some words and keep going, knowing that they can always revise later. When authors aren't sure how to describe a concept or idea, they give it their best shot and press on. When authors don't know what to write next, they just write something, *anything*. Authors do not write effortlessly. Quite the opposite, in fact.

Authors are the ones who just keep typing, day after day, year after year. It gets easier with time, but authors put in their 10,000 hours,[1] just like everyone else. Usually, we don't find out

[1] Gladwell, Malcolm. *Outliers: The Story of Success.* 2008. Little, Brown and Company: New York, NY.

about an author until she's already had great success. Agatha Christie received rejection letters for five years between finishing her first book and seeing it published. Five years! She went on to publish 91 books, amassing over $2 billion in book sales and gaining her the *Guinness Book of World Records* title of World's Bestselling Author.[2] We focus so easily on the author's success, but what we don't see is all of the years of writing toil *before* that success.

Myth: Authors have a lot of free time. They get up, have a leisurely day that involves a lot of walks, sessions of perusing the bookstore, coffee breaks three times a day, and hours to just sit and think.

Truth: Most successful authors began their writing career in the margins of their normal life. John Grisham was a full-time lawyer, so he would be at the office at 5 am in order to get two hours of writing in before starting work.[3] Danielle Steel wrote late at night and usually only slept for four hours so she could spend time with her children during the day.[4]

I haven't reached the heights of Grisham or Steel, but I'm using them as inspiration in my own writing schedule. I'm writing this book while

---

[2] Curran, John. 75 Facts about Christie. AgathaChristie.com.

[3] Academy of Achievement: John Grisham Interview. Achievement.org.

[4] Angel, Karen. Lonely Heart. The Age. March 18, 2011. The Age.com.

my four-month-old daughter lies next to me on the couch. She's just had her first 30-minute feed (at 5 am), and now I have 30 minutes before my other two children wake up. Then, we all have school, work, and normal, busy lives through the rest of the day. At 5:30 am, when I'm tempted to go back to bed ("just for a few minutes!"), I remind myself that true authors are willing to make a book happen in small chunks of time and in the margins of life.

As E.B. White said, "A writer who waits for ideal conditions under which to work will die without putting a word on paper."[5]

Myth: To be a successful author, you have to write every single day.

Truth: I have heard this excuse a lot: "I can't write every day, so I don't think I could ever be a real author." Yes, some authors do write every day, but that's not what makes them successful. What makes them successful is they're committed, whatever their schedule. Some write a little every day. Stephen King writes at least 2,000 words a day.[6] Some write for several hours a few times a week. Tom Pollock writes on Monday nights, Wednesday nights, and during the day on Sundays.[7] Some write for weeks straight only a few

---

5 Plimpton, George, and Crowther, Frank H. The Art of the Essay No. 1, E.B. White. *The Paris Review*. TheParisReview.org.

6 King, Stephen. *On Writing: A Memoir of the Craft*. 2000. Scribner: New York, NY.

7 Pollack, Tom: Writing Around a Day Job. TerribleMinds. August

times a year. Nathan Lowell doesn't write for months at a time, then will write 10,000 to 20,000 words a day while working on a manuscript.[8]

Don't use your schedule as an excuse. So you really can't write every day? How often *can* you write? Pick some times every week, or some days every month, or some weeks every year that you can write. Commit.

Myth: Successful authors get published because they have special connections with agents or publishers, or someone in the know.

Truth: There have always been ways around the "big publishers," if you're dedicated to getting your book out there. Beginning in the late 1800s,[9] there were "vanity" publishing houses, which allowed writers to pay their own way to publication. (Lewis Carroll published *Alice's Adventures in Wonderland*, using his own money and a vanity press.[10]) Throughout the 1900s, independent publishing houses became more popular and more profitable, especially with the technology to mass-produce paperbacks in the 1950s[11]. Today, with the internet,

---

11, 2004. TerribleMinds.com.

8 Penn, Joanna. Writing Every Day vs. Binge Writing. The Creative Penn. February 23, 2011. TheCreativePenn.com

9 The Society for the History of Authorship, Reading and Publishing. Sharpweb.org.

10 Maeda, Martha. *Book Publishing 101: Inside Information to Getting Your First Book or Novel Published.* 2004. Atlantic Publishing Group, Inc.: Starke, FL.

11 The Society for the History of Authorship, Reading and Publishing. Sharpweb.org.

getting published is as easy as uploading a document to Amazon.

Getting published isn't and never has been the problem. What savvy authors worry about is getting people to buy their book. The truth is that even if you get a book contract with a traditional publisher, big publishers put out more than a book a week, and they usually only have a few publicists, so they can't publicize every book effectively. Publishing houses have always put most of their marketing firepower behind authors who have already sold well. So, it has always been an unfair market for the first-time author. It was unfair for Carroll and Rowling. And it'll be unfair for you, too.

That said, book marketing is changing drastically. The number of people who speak English, are literate, and have internet access increases constantly. Your potential readership is larger than it ever has been. You don't need connections to publish. In reality, there's a huge market already out there, just waiting for your book.

Myth: For a writer to become a first-time author, you have to be willing to spend a lot of money, like tens of thousands of dollars.

Truth: You are going to spend some money, but it won't be a fortune, especially when you consider the benefits of publishing. If you're going the self-publishing route (and I would highly recommend that you consider it), and assuming you already have a computer, you're looking at spending a total of $2,500–$5,000 on an editor, a proofreader, a book cover artist, a formatter, and possibly a marketing professional.[12]

Honestly, though, even if you are able to land a traditional publisher, you'll still spend money out of pocket on some editing and publicity. (First-time authors do a lot of their own marketing, even if they're working with traditional publishers.) You may recoup some of your losses in sales of the book, or you may recoup them in increased business, speaking gigs, new clients, new joint venture opportunities—who knows!

That's the exciting part of writing a book: you never know what doors it'll open. Yes, it's an upfront investment—not a fortune—but the rewards could be huge.

Myth: Successful authors are rolling in money.

Truth: A few authors make a ton of money on their book sales. You know the big names: successful authors including Bill Bryson, Malcolm Gladwell, John Grisham, David McCullough, James Patterson, Tony Robbins, J.K. Rowling, and Danielle Steel. While those people make a lot of money on book sales, most authors don't. They spend a lot of time marketing their book;

[12] For my own book, I spent about $1,000 on editing, $800 on the cover, and $400 on proofreading and formatting. But if you need more help with editing or additional formatting for printed book, you'll need to budget a bit more.

arguably, that means the book profits just pay for their time spent doing that, so they can keep writing.

Think about it. If it takes you 200 hours to write and revise the book, plus 50–100 hours on the actual publishing (art, layout, formatting), not to mention hundreds of hours on marketing (radio shows, podcasts, blogs, TV shows, and book signings), you'd have to make a lot of money on a book to earn even minimum wage back on 500+ hours. Authors don't do it for the money—they do it for the opportunities.

So, if you're hoping to churn out a quick e-book, make a ton of cash, and never write another day in your life, this book may not be for you. I'm here to talk to the person who wants to write, feels drawn to writing and has a message to share, is willing to put in some long hours, but just doesn't have a clue how to start.

I'm talking to you because you've been lied to about the writing process. Some lies make writing sound harder than it actually is. Some lies make it sound easier than it actually is. Now that we've separated some fact from fiction, let's talk about you writing your book.

One undeniable truth: You can write a book.

Whoever you are, you can write a book. If you have terrible grammar, you can write a book. If you only have chunks of 10–15 minutes throughout the day, you can write a book. If you only have a vague idea of what you want to write and an insatiable calling to write *something*, you can write a book. If you have no real connections in publishing and no fortune to spend on your writing, you can write a book. Heck, even if you have arthritis and can't type, you can write a book. (Ever heard of transcribers? That's right. You talk, they type. You can write a book.)

I'm not saying it'll be easy. I'm saying it's possible.

It's your own mindset that prevents you from writing your book.

We pour too much of our irreplaceable time and energy into these old myths about what it takes to be a successful author. How many times have you sat in front of a laptop screen, unable to find the right words, and you're thinking to yourself some version of these myths? "I just don't have the God-given talent that other writers do." Maybe, "If I just had more time, I could get my thoughts straight and write." Or, "Even if I do write a book, no one's ever going to read it because I don't have any connections in the publishing industry."

Every minute that you allow your brain to turn those thoughts over and over again is a minute of wasted time and energy that you could have been using to write your book.

Instead of letting your thoughts focus on what you don't have, direct your thoughts to something more useful—namely, why you want to write your book in the first place.

Look, writing a book is a battle. That battle will be won or lost in your own head. If you believe that writing is something only for special people with lots of time, talent, connections, and money, I can tell you right now that you'll never write a book.

But, if you believe that anyone can write a book, that anyone can gather their thoughts into words, put them on paper, and shape them into something that helps other people, then you have just taken your first step toward success.

The best way to win the mental battle of writing is to constantly redirect your thoughts to why you're writing your book. Let's talk about some of the good, worthwhile reasons to write a book.

You're just curious: Maybe you feel a mysterious tug, a curiosity that keeps recurring in your mind. Even though you try to put aside the thought of writing a book, it just keeps coming back to you, almost like a challenge. Can you do it? You'll never know if you don't try, and part of you wants to give it a go.

You want to help others: Maybe you have some knowledge, advice, or experience that you think would be useful to a group of people. Perhaps you've worked in an industry for many years and come up with ways to improve how it works. Perhaps you've had some hard times in life, learned a lot of lessons along the way, and you want to pass on the advice you wish someone had given you years ago. Perhaps you've had some experience in life that you simply feel needs to be shared. All of these are great reasons to write a book, and helping others is always a worthy cause.

You want to tell your story: Some of the best conversations occur when we sit down and give space for the other person to tell her story—not just the bullet points version or the history plotted on a timeline version, but the fleshed-out-in-all-its-glory-and-gore version. When a friend bares her story and lets us truly see how she has come to be who she is, there is a true, palpable connection.

We can feel the same way when we read someone's story in a book. Words are powerful, whether written or spoken. If you have the sense that your story could touch someone else's life in a powerful way, well, that's one of the best reasons there is to write a book.

You have a business: If you serve clients or develop products, you have some expertise. Maybe you shrug your shoulders instinctively when I say, "You have expertise," like you want to brush off what you're capable of, but it's true. The best way to lay claim to that expertise, to live in it, to truly recognize it, and to share it with others is to write a book. A book establishes you as an expert in the field. Every field has experts. If you aren't claiming your space as one of them, then you're allowing others to fill that gap. Wouldn't it be better for the world if you stepped in and laid claim to that talent of yours?

You want to start a business: You don't have

to wait until you have clients or a product before you write a book. A book can be one of the best ways to attract new clients. If you feel the urge, don't wait. Go ahead and write the book! It'll pave the way for your business.

You have a message: Maybe you aren't sure that a book is the only way to spread your message. You bounce back and forth between starting a blog, writing a book, recording a podcast, shooting YouTube videos, or just going out and talking to people. None of them are mutually exclusive! I would recommend pursuing whatever options you feel are good for you, but know that writing a book could take a while, so go ahead and start writing anyway.

Any other reasons? Tell me, why did you pick up this book? You must have a book idea in your head and a reason to start writing. I would love to hear your reason. Really! Share your book idea and why you want to write a book by emailing me at morgan@morgangistmacdonald.com.

CHAPTER TWO

Preventing self-sabotage

At first, you'll be excited to write your book. You'll wake up early, skip lunch, stay up late. Your book will call to you during the day, and you won't be able to stop thinking about it—like a bad high school crush.

But after the newness wears off (anywhere from three days to three weeks), you'll start to have this trapped, constricted feeling. You'll want to put off writing the book, but you'll feel guilty. Suddenly, the project will take on a life of its own, like it's forcing you to work on it. Then, you'll start to foster some resentment, and procrastination will beckon even more. You won't be able to shake the feeling of guilt.

You'll begin to self-sabotage your progress. You'll stay up late watching TV, and then you'll justify hitting the snooze button and skipping your morning writing session. You'll have work deadlines closing in, so you'll eat lunch at your desk, rather than escaping for a 25-minute writing session. You'll decide responding to emails is more urgent than writing your book.

Once self-sabotage kicks in, it's extremely difficult to escape. But you *can* prevent self-sabotage, with a few mindset shifts.

Stay connected with your why

It is crucial to remind yourself constantly why this book is important to you. In the grand scheme of things, writing a book is completely voluntary. It's what crazy people do. There are plenty of other ways to make money, tell your story, and gain prestige. It's tempting to just drop the whole book idea entirely.

The only way you'll be able to write and finish your book is if you continually remind yourself why you wanted to write the book in the first place. Zero in on the irreplaceable, irrefutable, undeniable reason why this book on this topic matters to you right now. Write down your reason why in one to three sentences. Read it every single time you sit down to write. Tape it to your screen, mirror, coffee pot, or TV, if you need to remind yourself why you want to write your book instead of checking email or turning on the news.

When you're first sitting down to write your "why this book is important to me" sentences, pay attention to your own emotions. If it takes you a long time to come up with a good reason, or if you feel weighed down and trapped when you're posting your why above your workspace, that's a problem.

Writing and posting your why should lift your spirits and inspire you. Writing is a draining process, and it's easy to lose sight of why we should return to our screens day after day, typing words that no one is reading... yet. Reconnecting with your why is the only way you're going to convince yourself to open your document again and type some more words.

If you try to write out your why and post it, but feel a sense of dread, obligation, or dryness, then stop and re-evaluate. Maybe you *do* want to write a book but maybe not *this* book. You might pick a book topic because it makes logical sense, but your heart isn't really in it. If you're trying to write a book because someone said you should, but you're not excited by the idea, you might as well stop right now. That book project will be nothing but pain and drudgery for you. And you'll likely never finish.

On the other hand, if you write out your why statement, post it above your workspace and immediately feel a lift, an energy pooling inside of you—*that* is a good indication that you're starting a project in line with who you are, what you hope for, and where you're going in life. You'll use that pool of energy every day to finish your book. So, listen carefully to your emotions as you think through and write out why you're writing your book.

Writing out your why in one to three sentences is key. Don't skip this step. Don't talk yourself into believing that "thinking" about your why is the same as writing it. One to three complete sentences, written out, posted somewhere visible. Coach's orders!

What are my why sentences? Here's what's posted on my laptop, where I do all of my writing:

"I am writing this book to encourage and inspire writers to stop procrastinating and to give them the tools to write their book. This book will change some writer's life; she'll write the book she's always wanted, and that book might just change the world. This book will also help me connect with authors and grow my business, so that I'm able to support my family and work from anywhere in the world."

Notice how my why includes how I'll help others and how I'll help myself. That's not selfish. Your book will benefit others' lives, as well as your own life. That's how the best and most worthwhile projects work—it's a win-win, all the way around.

Gather support

You'll need to strategically pull people into your writing process. You probably want to hide in a dark corner, write when no one's looking, and wait until the manuscript is "in a good place" before showing it to anyone. But it'll be a long, lonely writing process if you operate like that.

Recruit at least one person who will support you unconditionally, someone who believes in you like you wish you believed in yourself, someone you can go to for words of hope when you feel the doubts suffocating you. This person is entirely for moral support, the type of person who will read anything you've written and love it—an encourager.

For me, this is my mom. When I tell her that I'm writing something, she always asks how it's going, out of a very genuine desire to know about something that's important to me. She'll gladly read anything I write and find something positive about it. I could write 20,000 words of gibberish, and she would say, "You're really making good progress! That's a lot of words."

But you'll need a second type of support, as well—someone who will give you thoughtful, constructive, specific, even negative feedback on your manuscript. This is like your alpha reader. People often bring in beta readers after they've finished a manuscript, to get people's opinions on what they've written. I'm suggesting you bring in an alpha reader—the person who reads drafts when you aren't even close to finishing the project. This person will read a rough draft and see the potential in it, but he will also point out areas that you need to work on, clarify, maybe even leave out entirely.

For me, this is my husband. Of course, he offers me moral support, but he will also give feedback about what could be different or better. Sometimes I bristle against the feedback (we'll talk more about how to take criticism in later), but his suggestions are always rooted in his desire to make the piece better. That's *exactly* what you need in an alpha reader.

Could your encourager and your alpha reader be the same person? Absolutely, if you're lucky enough to have a person like that in your life. If you don't have an encourager or an alpha reader in your life, you might think about a writing coach or an editor. Yes, you can bring people into your writing project before it's finished. I know that as a writing coach, it's always my goal to be both unconditionally supportive and provide feedback that will help the author bring the manuscript to its fullest potential.

Allow yourself to be a writer

Before you even start writing, you need to start thinking of yourself as a writer and allow it to become part of your identity. If selling a million copies of a book were a requirement to being called a writer, no one would ever become a writer. You are a writer when you commit to writing—plain and simple. Give yourself the title, and claim it.

Commit to writing 5,000 words per week. You can write 1,000 words five days a week or 750 words seven days a week or 5,000 words on a Saturday afternoon—whatever works best in *your* life. No one way is better than another. But you have to commit *before* you sit down to write. I promise, 75 percent of the time, you will come up with convincing excuses about why you can't write today; why you'd rather wait until tomorrow. Do *not* let yourself get away with these excuses. Sure, you might miss a writing day now and then, but if you do, you'd better make up the word count by the end of the week. And if you fall short of 5,000 one week, make it up the next week.

Are you ready to commit to writing regularly? Do you believe you can write this book? I believe you can. And I believe you are a writer. So, let's start writing, shall we?

CHAPTER THREE

Good writing habits

Habits—don't they seem like the holy grail of life? If only you had the habit of running every day, you'd be in shape. If only you had the habit of meditating every day, you'd be a calmer, saner person. If only you had the habit of grocery shopping regularly, you'd eat more healthfully. If only you had the habit of reading every day, you'd have better mental focus. If only you had the habit of writing every day, you'd be an author by now.

So, you try to adopt one new habit. (Or two. Or five.). And yet, a week or two in, you let the habit slide, and you never quite recover. What's missing? Your commitment to focusing on the habit as your priority.

Let's have a heart-to-heart here. You bought

this book, you've read the first few chapters, you've probably already started to write. (Perhaps on more than one occasion?) You need more than just an interest in writing a book. You need to *commit* to writing a book. You don't have to write productively and prolifically every day for the rest of your life to be a writer. You can commit to seasons and spurts. Let's face it. Not many of us achieve that longed-for perfect balance of writing every day, reading every day, meditating every day, running every day, and cooking three meals every day. Such perfect balance simply isn't achievable—at least not all at once—so we focus on one or a few areas of life at a time.

I'd suggest you should pick writing to focus on for this upcoming season of life and just go for it.

It's decision time—right here, right now.

Do you want to write a book, or don't you?

Do you want to commit the next few months of your life to getting this book written, published, and into the hands of the people who need to read it?

If your answer is, "Not right now, but maybe later," put down this book, because it's not worth your time. When you're ready, you can always come back to it.

If your answer is, "Hell, yeah!" we've got something to work with.

A few key decisions now will make all the difference later on. Ready to tackle some tricky stuff? Let's talk about how you're going to write your book.

First, how long do you want your book to be? You could write a shorter 15,000–20,000 word e-book (that's 60–80 pages) in six weeks, easily. This sort of quick e-book is great for building your platform, growing your business, getting your message out to the world fast, and positioning yourself as an expert in your field. If you're going for a full-length manuscript, that'll probably be more like 50,000–70,000 words (200–280 pages). For something like this, you should plan for four months of writing. A longer book can help establish you as a true authority, someone who seriously knows her stuff about her field.

You may not have a clue how long you want the book to be yet, and that's okay. Plan for three months of writing. In three months, you can either finish a short book or be very close to finishing a full-length book. Can you change your life so that writing is your priority for the next three months? If you can, let's talk about specific habits you'll need to see your book all the way through to the finished manuscript.

Writing routines

There are several ways to think about how your writing should be a part of a routine. First, what devices you use for writing. Second, when and where you write. Third, the software that you use when writing.

Write on only one or two devices. With different desktops at home and at the office, laptops for travel, phones with Google Docs, and tablets with full writing software on them, it's tempting to just write wherever you happen to be, with whatever device you happen to have. Even analog writers often have a problem of a notebook at home, a smaller one to take in a bag, and grabbing bits of paper to jot down notes sporadically. Using different devices (or notebooks) is going to get very confusing, very quickly.

The underlying problem of wanting to write on different devices or in different notebooks is that you're probably not in an actual writing routine. I won't say that you have to write in the same place, at the same time every day, but you should have some rhythms around when and where you write. Let's set out the two different scenarios, and you can judge for yourself which is most likely to produce a book.

Scenario 1: You have a pretty fluid schedule, and you try to roll with what the week has to offer. Sometimes you write at your office computer during lunch. Other days you're busy, so you dictate notes to yourself while you drive home. If it was an activity-filled week with the kids, you might put the little ones to bed early and let the older ones watch a movie, while you sneak away with your laptop for a few minutes of writing time. On travel days, you might type out some notes on your tablet while waiting at the terminal. On a very rare productive morning, you decide to set the alarm early, wake up, and add notes on your laptop at the kitchen table.

Scenario 2: Your week can be pretty unpredictable, so you have a couple of times when you try to write. First, you aim to write in the morning, before the day gets going. You set an alarm and enjoy a cup of coffee while writing at the kitchen table. But, you're human, and sometimes the morning just doesn't work out. So, you have Back-up Plan A—writing at your office desktop during your lunch break. Of course, sometimes a co-worker invites you to lunch or there's a meeting, in which case you have Back-up Plan B, skipping the TV show before bed and writing for a few minutes on your laptop.

Both scenarios assume that you're a busy person. Believe me, I've never worked with an author who wasn't busy. Heck, I don't know that I've had a conversation with anyone in the last 10 years who didn't profess to be "crazy busy." Still, do you see the difference between Scenario 1 and Scenario 2? Sure, in Scenario 1, you may seem like you're squeezing writing time into every corner of your schedule (that's productive, right?) but your writing is bound to be scattered because you are writing on so many devices, in different physical places, at different times during the day. And there are no plans or intentions to try to write at given times. If you don't set expectations with yourself that you'll write at X time, in Y location, then you can't say that you didn't meet your goal. There was no goal. So it's easy to let yourself off the hook.

In Scenario 2, you see the benefit of having a

primary writing time, with the back-up plans, in case life gets busy. There's an expectation that you'll write in the morning, but if something happens, you'll know to check in with your schedule at lunchtime, and if the lunchtime writing doesn't happen, check in with yourself again prior to turning on the TV before bedtime. It's a straightforward way to know at the end of the day whether you met your goal of writing, and you'll know which part of the day didn't work out. Then, you can begin to notice patterns of when writing works best for you.

When establishing your writing routine, don't get hung up on the software you use for writing. Some people swear by certain software programs, and the software changes every few years. One year it's Microsoft Word, then Scrivener, then Google Docs. Let me assure you, the software is not nearly as important as your commitment to write regularly, on whatever you have available. For most of human history, books have been written with pen and paper, so don't fall into the trap of thinking that there's a huge difference between writing a book with one software package over another. No matter the interface, writing a book mostly amounts to you typing a heck of a lot of words into your computer.

If you decide to write your book long-hand or talk your book onto an audio recording device, I recommend you hire someone to convert your handwriting or your audio notes into typed notes. You can hire people online. The reason I say this?

Your focus must be spending your free time creating content, not typing up your own notes.

To establish a rhythmic writing routine, decide on one or two devices (or notebooks) for writing, and decide on some times in your day when you expect you'll be able to write consistently.

Free-writing

Throughout your book-writing journey, I recommend establishing a habit of free-writing. Most people think they know what free-writing is—that they just sit down and write what comes to mind—but free-writing is a structured technique of its own. Mark Levy's book *Accidental Genius: Using Writing to Generate Your Best Ideas, Insight, and Content*[13] gives an elaborate overview of free-writing, but let me sum up the technique for you.

Your brain has all the raw material you need for your writing. Your mind contains more thoughts, information, associations, and ideas than you could ever sort through, even with the most concerted effort. When you dream, when you cross a familiar intersection, when you smell bacon early in the morning, these situations bring about memories and thoughts completely without your intention. Levy argues that many

---

[13] Levy, Mark. *Accidental Genius: Using Writing to Generate Your Best Ideas, Insight, and Content.* 2010. Berrett-Koehler Publishers, Inc.: San Francisco, CA.

(perhaps most) of your thoughts cannot be accessed through sheer will.

When we sit down to write a book, though, many of us try to do exactly that, shoving our words out, using brute force, willing ourselves to access those very ideas and thoughts. We end up sitting in front of the computer, hands poised... motionless. After five minutes, we give up and remain frustrated for the rest of the day. Is there a way to tap into this mine of raw material at a particular time and place, like during your morning writing session at the kitchen table? Yes, there is.

Free-writing pushes your brain to think longer, deeper, and more unconventionally than it normally would. Free-writing is essentially a form of forced creativity that actually works.

Here are the basic steps:

1. Set a timer for 5, 10, or 20 minutes.
2. Hands to pen and paper or keyboard, whichever your preference.
3. Pick a prompt, if you like, or just set your mind at ease.
4. Write as fast as reasonably possible—no pauses, no breaks, no breathers—for the full allotment of the time. Resist hitting the delete or backspace key. (That one's hard for me.) If you can't think of the right word, just keep typing letters or "umm umm umm"

> until it comes to you, or repeating the most recent word over and over again "again again again again." And then when you're ready to move on, type that word and keep going.

If you reach the end of a sentence, start asking yourself questions, "Why do I think that way? Why is that the best thing to talk about in the book? If that's true, what else is true? If that's true, is the opposite false?" Type questions and answers to yourself. Don't look back, don't delete, don't correct spelling mistakes. Press on until the timer rings.

The key to free-writing is to write as fast as you possibly can.

The goal here is to physically push past your internal editor. You have a million ideas swimming about in your brain, drifting, colliding, generally being useless. You need to get those ideas down onto paper so you can think about them properly. The problem is your internal editor has a habit of stopping those ideas before you manage to type them out. The thought flits across your brain, but your fingers are paused at the keyboard, and you think, "No, I'm not going to write that."

In this exercise, it'll be too late for your internal editor to stop you. You'll be writing so dang fast that your brain won't even know what's happened. And as you're writing this utter gobbledy-gook nonsense, you will stumble upon the most brilliant ideas—ideas that never would have made it on to the paper had you not been typing so fast.

You must do your best to type faster than you think. And you have to keep typing until your timer rings. You finish that last thought and stop once the timer rings. You're forming a pact with your internal editor. "I will push past you because I'm typing at lightning speed, but I will only push past you for 20 minutes. Then, you may regain control." After a few sessions, your internal editor will relax, knowing that it's only 20 minutes. If you push past the 20 minutes, you negate that pact. In fact, it's quite difficult to maintain that speed for more than 30 minutes anyway. (I can't do 30. I top out at 20.) So, give yourself a break as soon as the timer rings.

Here are some helpful ground rules that Levy gives:

> **Try easy.** Levy emphasizes that you have to set your mind at ease. No one will read your free-writing. Don't expect words of genius to fall from your pen like rain from a cloud. Give yourself permission to simply write, with no expectations that this writing will ever produce anything useful.
>
> **Write fast and continuously.** Typically, when you're writing, I imagine you think at a much slower pace than normal. Try to push your brain closer to a normal rate of thought, which will probably feel approximately twice as fast as

your typical "writing rate." The goal here is not high-quality words or even fully formed thoughts. The goal is to push past your internal editor. If you're writing faster than your internal editor, then you're beginning to tap into the raw material that's waiting in the recesses of your mind. If you're not writing as fast as you reasonably can, though, you won't be able to tap into that raw material.

Work against a limit. Using a timer keeps you focused and reassures you that you only have to keep up this uncomfortably fast pace for a short period of time. You can do anything for 5, 10, or 20 minutes. Write for the full time allotment. Then stop as soon as that timer rings. In order for your mind to get comfortable with free-writing, you have to strike the bargain with yourself, "I'll write for 20 minutes at an accelerated pace, but *only* for 20 minutes."

If you get to the end of an idea, ask yourself a new question. Sometimes you'll reach the end of a particular thought, hit the "." key, and not know which way to turn. This is free-writing, though. You're not required to write in a linear, logical pattern. Pick a new question, a new thought, a new problem, and just keep writing.

When people say they're "writing," what they often mean is that they're sitting in front of their computer, staring at the screen, while a thousand thoughts run through their mind, none of them useful for the piece at hand. Free-writing helps you sift through all of those random thoughts and put a messy tangle of them down into words. Some of those thoughts will be fruitful for the writing, but some of those thoughts you just need to get out of your head and out of the way before you can truly begin.

This is why some people get caught up in organizing their desks, to-do lists, or physical spaces. There's a jumbled disaster of thoughts in their head. Instead of sitting down to sort out those thoughts, straight on, they putter with some other organizational technique. But cleaning your desk for 15 minutes is not nearly as effective as writing for 15 minutes. Even combing through your notes on your book topic for 15 minutes is not as effective as free-writing for that time.

It's important to establish a regular routine of clearing out the mess of thoughts with free-writing before you sit down to write. Believe me, I know this is not easy. Even I am sometimes lured by the thought of productivity. I think, "I only have 30 minutes to write. I should spend all of that time on my book." Inevitably, I spend 15 minutes dawdling and doodling. Really, I should spend 15 minutes free-writing and 15 minutes writing on the book—that way, the 15 minutes spent writing on the book would be more useful and powerful.

Use a timer

All this talk of 15 minutes here and 25 minutes there reminds me—one of the most important tools for a productive writer is a timer. A writer's greatest battle is achieving and maintaining focus. Nothing kick starts focus like setting a timer. Whatever you're doing as a writer—free-writing, researching, drafting—do it all with a timer running.

Perhaps you've heard of the Pomodoro technique? In his book, *The Pomodoro Technique,*[14] Francesco Cirillo advises you to work in small chunks of time with short breaks in between. The easiest way to start is to work for a 25-minute chunk, break for five minutes, and work for another 25-minute chunk. You set your intention for work before you start the timer, so not a second is wasted on "What will I work on now?" You decide what you'll focus on, you hit the timer, and your focus begins to align with action right away. It's a bit miraculous, really.

Some authors claim that they need anywhere from two to six hours to get any proper writing done. I would challenge them to show how many words they've written at the end of six hours. From my experience, unless you're on a tight, looming deadline, you're probably only going to write a few thousand words in any one day, no matter how many hours you devote to writing.

---

[14] Cirillo, Francesco. *The Pomodoro Technique: Do More and Have Fun with Time Management*. www.FCGarage.com.

In fact, I'd argue that the same author who claims he needs six hours to write productively could get the same amount of writing down in six Pomodoro sessions. That's three hours, broken down like this:

25 minutes of writing (500 words)
5-minute break
25 minutes of writing (500 words)
5-minute break
25 minutes of writing (500 words)
5-minute break
25 minutes of writing (500 words)
5-minute break
25 minutes of writing (500 words)
5-minute break
25 minutes of writing (500 words)
5-minute break

That estimate of writing 500 words in 25 minutes is based on a rough average of my own and my clients' writing pace. My pace is more like 1,000 words in 25 minutes, but I do practice a lot. Relatively speaking, though, 500 words in 25 minutes is definitely attainable by an average person. Altogether, 3,000 words—which is roughly 12 pages—is quite a lot of writing for one day.

If, however, you devoted six hours to writing, it's easy to see how you'd waste a lot of that time, simply because you *feel* like you have all day. You'd sit down at your desk, putter around, clean up, maybe do a few administrative tasks. You might review some of your notes and previous writing. It may be an hour before you get anything down on the page. You'd write for maybe an hour, with spurts of productivity, then break for water or a snack for 15–20 minutes.

Then you'd write for maybe an hour, starting to get your pace established. Then you'd break for lunch, which might add up to 45 minutes. If you're good at keeping yourself on task, you'd get another hour of writing in, but then your focus would probably wane, and you'd find yourself puttering around once again. In a six-hour day, I would bet you would typically spend three hours writing, and not all of that time will be nose-to-the-grindstone, productive writing.

It's much better to do six sessions of the Pomodoro technique, and you could finish roughly the same amount of writing in three hours.

In general, I don't recommend that you wait around until life hands you a full day, or even a half day, to start writing. It'll take you years to write the book, and you'll forget much of what you've written in between sessions. Keep a steady clip of short sessions, and the whole writing process will go much more smoothly.

The exception: If you have a hard deadline approaching, adrenaline can do wonders for your focus. If your manuscript is due to the publisher in one week, and you still have 30,000 words to write, you sure as heck can get a lot of writing done in one week—if you shut yourself off from the world.

It all ultimately comes down to your focus. But don't lie to yourself. It's incredibly difficult to focus on writing for more than three hours in a day. Instead of waiting to write two to three hours once a week, I'd recommend you use the Pomodoro technique to write one or two 25-minute sessions regularly throughout the week. You'll keep up pace, momentum, and you won't forget what you were writing nearly as easily.

Create weekly word count goals and track your progress

As a former teacher of college students and now a coach for writers, I've seen the same productivity patterns play out for 18-year-olds writing a term paper due in one week as for authors writing a book due in one month. There's a sudden adrenaline rush, and all of those nebulous "I don't know what I'm writing about" ideas collide harshly and coalesce, somehow, into a written work.

When time feels expansive and unhurried, we procrastinate. We dilly-dally. We write a bit here and there, but we waste minutes and hours on pointless, needless tasks.

Then, time contracts. We see the calendar deadline looming, reminding us that our writing is due, that there will be some external consequence if we don't finish our writing. That's when the productivity kicks in. Suddenly, we're cranking out 3,000 words in a day, writing with a furious intensity, as if our lives (or at least the meaning in our lives) depended on it.

In these days of constricted time and intense productivity, we find that we can shift our lives around for at least a few days to get some serious writing done. We alter the normal progress of our day. We wake up earlier, stay up later, tell friends we can't meet up for dinner, ask family to babysit the kids for a while, ask our spouses to pick up some extra slack—just for a few days.

What if we could harness the power of these two methods of writing to create a blend of focused daily productivity and powerful productive burst?

Here's the method that I've discovered works best. (If you know yourself and feel the need to tweak this method, then by all means do so!)

Set weekly word count goals. If you work and have a family, 5,000 words per week is ambitious but not crazy. A pokey writer can peck out 500 words an hour, so that's a max of 10 hours of writing per week. A faster writer can type 1,000 words an hour, which would be five hours of writing per week. Someone who writes on a regular basis can often crank out 2,000 words an hour, so that's two to three hours of writing per week. Even if you begin as the pokey sort, you'll soon pick up the pace. If writing your book is important to you, you can carve out five to 10 hours of writing per week.

Track your word count progress. I like to use an Excel spreadsheet. In fact, I use Google Sheets, so I can easily share my progress with others. (Accountability—we'll get to that.) Devise a system that captures the date, day of the week, time, length of writing session, word count, and any miscellaneous notes. At the end of each week, the idea is you're able to write whether you met your word count goal and what your goal is for the following week.

Take a look in Appendix B for my Google Sheet that tracked my progress for this book and a Bonus Worksheet to help you create your own sheet to track your progress.

You could also use a calendar. You could use a Word document. You could use Post-its, note cards, a chalkboard. Whatever you want. Just be sure to track your progress.

Even though tracking your progress is absolutely vital, it feels like a pain in the moment, and you think, "Well, I have a pretty good idea of how I'm doing with my progress." However, a week from now, you won't. You'll forget which mornings were best for you to get up, you'll overestimate or underestimate how many words you write in a 25-minute chunk, and you'll lose sight of how far you've come.

Without tracking, we tend to overestimate our progress. We think, "Oh yeah, I'm doing great. I write a bit here and there, making it one step at a time." In reality, we may barely clear 1,000 words a week. At that pace, it would take 60 weeks (that's one year and two months!) to write a *first draft* of a full-length book. And that's if you're writing every single week. Tracking your progress helps you see when you think you're making progress, but really you're languishing.

Other people will tend to underestimate their progress. They'll insult themselves, thinking, "I'm not being productive enough. I never get enough writing time. At this pace, I'll never finish this book." But, all the while, they're clearing 5,000 words per week. They're on track to finish a full-length book in three months.

People who underestimate their progress also sometimes have the issue of producing high word count with no real direction. It's not enough to write for hours every week; you have to write with some sort of purpose. Tracking your progress will help you see if you've written 20,000 words but haven't finished the first chapter. (Side note: That's a problem that would require some reorganization. If you find yourself in that boat, skip to the reverse outline section in "Beyond the first draft." Create a reverse outline of your directionless 20,000 words, and that should bring in some clarity.)

A tool, like a Google Sheet, is useful to remind us how we're progressing. But let's face it, we're really good at excusing ourselves when we don't make the kind of progress we'd set out to initially. We tell ourselves, "This last week was particularly unusual. My kid was sick. There was a time change. I had a busy week at work." All of the excuses may be totally legitimate (and that increases their power over us), so even if we're tracking our progress, it's only as useful to us as we allow it to be.

Accountability

It's also important to bring other people into your progress. Oh yes, it's scary to admit out loud to someone that you're writing a book. Just that phrase "I'm writing a book" seems to have airs that you're some sort of expert, that you know something other people don't, that you can describe people or emotions or events in a way that's extraordinarily moving. How presumptuous it sounds to say, "I'm writing a book!"

If you don't bring at least one person into your project—someone who will hold you accountable to the progress you want to make—you will not finish your book.

Let's unpack a bit why you might be nervous to bring on an accountability partner.

You may feel that people who write books are experts, so if you tell someone else you're writing a book, you feel like you're proclaiming that you somehow understand things better than others. There are two ways I would encourage you to re-examine this belief.

First, everyone is an expert at something. You don't have to have a Ph.D. to be an expert (as much as academia would like to perpetuate that myth). My sister is an expert at planning trips around the world, where she has an outgoing plane ticket, a return plane ticket, and a backpack.

She has a wealth of knowledge and experience with traveling light, without a set itinerary. My landscape man is an expert at how to treat plants in Houston weather. He tells me when to trim Crepe myrtles, when to turn off my sprinkler system because the ground is too damp, and what kinds of plants will grow with the least attention.

In my mind, both of these people are experts because I turn to them for advice all the time. If I were to ask one of them to write a book, I bet both would say, "But I'm not an expert! There are hundreds of people who know more about travel [or yard maintenance] than I do." Maybe, but I turn to *you* for advice, so that means there's a segment of the world that doesn't have knowledge that you have. Meaning? There's space for your book.

Second, you don't have to wait until you're already an expert before you start writing a book; you *become* an expert *as* you write the book. If you did all the research necessary to become an "expert" in a field before you wrote a single word, you'd have an enormous amount of knowledge crammed in your brain, and it would take you forever to write your book. (Trust me, I've coached this type of expert author before!) It's a much smoother process, and very typical, to become an expert in an area as you research and write about it, all simultaneously. They say you learn a concept best when you teach it. You become an expert on a topic fastest when you write a book about it.

So, don't let the fact that you're not an expert keep you from pulling in an accountability partner. Everyone has a niche to speak of, and you become an expert along the way.

What else keeps us from bringing in an accountability partner?

Fear that we'll fail or just never complete our manuscript. If we keep it to ourselves or we keep accountability at a distance with conversations that start with, "I'm sort of writing a book, have been on and off for a few years," then we're holding ourselves back from committing, just in case it turns out we don't have what it takes to finish what we started. We hope no one will be disappointed, because no one knew or expected anything of us or our writing.

But, if you don't bring an accountability partner in, you absolutely will not finish your book. You are sabotaging your potential by keeping the project to yourself. You're afraid that you won't finish, so you do the *one* thing that absolutely will prevent you from finishing.

Decide right now who you're going to bring in as an accountability partner—someone who is generous, who believes in you, and who will remind you of the progress you wanted to make.

Call or email that person, and do it now. Tell him you're writing a book, even if you aren't sure what about yet, and tell him you'll get back to him with more details, but you'd be grateful if he could hold you accountable to making progress on writing the book.

Set aside time with your accountability partner to specifically talk about your book, at least once a month, at most once a week. It all depends on how fast you want to move through your manuscript. If you're writing 5,000 words per week, you'll have plenty to talk about once a week. If you're only writing 1,000 words or so per week, you might not have that much new progress to share, except once a month. If you're not sure what your pace is going to be, start with every other week and adjust up or down from there.

Not every friend is going to make a stellar accountability partner. If the person you originally choose flakes out or doesn't seem to care about your book, find another one. The accountability partner may be the only reason you finish your book, but you are still responsible for finding a partner who will serve your book well. If you ask someone to be your accountability partner who you know is going to cancel your coffee chats at the last second every time and you stick with that partner, it's absolutely your fault (not hers!) for choosing someone you knew wouldn't pull through.

Capture your spontaneous ideas

Last tip on this topic—and such common advice yet so often ignored. Develop a system to catch ideas on the fly. Once the book is entrenched in your thinking, you'll find yourself hit with bolts of inspiration at the most inconvenient times—

driving the kids to school, at the grocery store, putting gas in your car. Find a way to capture these jolts of inspiration.

I have Evernote on my phone, which is a cloud-based note-making application, so I can access the notes from my laptop when I'm sitting down to write. There are hundreds of other note-taking apps, including some very good ones that come standard to your phone, tablet, or computer. Some people use physical notebooks. Don't spend too much time analyzing the options. Just pick something and go with it. You can always adjust and grow into a new system later.

Recap and prioritize

I would say that all of these good writing habits are important, but it's tough to turn your life around in an instant. If I were to prioritize the habits, I would suggest you focus on:

1. Setting a weekly word count goal and creating a system to track your progress (even if it's just a piece of paper at first).
2. Establishing your writing routines by deciding when and where you'll be writing, and on what devices.
3. Free-writing before each writing session.
4. Using a timer to write in 25-minute chunks, with breaks in between.
5. Finding an accountability partner.

I put finding an accountability partner last because you want your partner to take you seriously. If you sign up an accountability partner, and you spend the first coffee chat complaining about how you're confused by writing on six different devices, do you think that person's going to feel sorry for you? Probably not. If you complain about not having ideas or time to write, your accountability partner might suddenly not have ideas or time for you, either. If you want your accountability partner to hold you to progress, you should have word count goals and a system for tracking progress already in place. The accountability partner is extremely important to the book-writing process, but you have to put your own mindset and systems in place first.

If *you* commit to taking your book seriously, other people will, too. Now you're prepped and ready to start writing your first draft. This next chapter will show you each phase of writing a first draft, from organization through coming up with a title.

CHAPTER FOUR

Writing the first draft

We've talked about writing habits, the ideals, what you *should* do when you're writing. Let's talk about sitting down to bang out that first draft.

There is one thing that all successful writers have in common: They dedicate time to putting words on the page. It's that simple. It's that terrifyingly simple.

We so easily talk ourselves into thinking that we need a certain computer setup, a particular amount of free time, an especially good idea, and just the right habits. Those are admirable ambitions (and part of my reason for writing this book). Yet nothing—absolutely nothing—can replace time spent putting words on a page.

You have to reach the point where you're

ready to push past the fear, past the excuses, past the uncertainty and self-doubt, open up a blank page, and start typing.

How do you make a start? What do you write first? I'll break down my recommendations for authors. Ultimately, how to write your first draft is a philosophy; everyone has their own system that they tweak. Every author I work with takes my system and adjusts it to her own style. I recommend you do the same.

I suggest following a process that looks something like this:

- Create a timeline (1 day)
- Free-write on the topic (1 week)
- Draft the rough organization (1 week)
- Write the first draft (3–7 weeks)
- Write the introduction and title (1 day)

Create a timeline

This will be a timeline for the entire book, from first draft to finished manuscript, based on how many words per week you believe you can write. Admittedly, it's a bit arbitrary to set a timeline for a project you haven't started yet. The goal is to set a reasonable timeline, with a challenging deadline, and (worst comes to worst) you readjust as you go. Without a deadline, though, you'll have no reason to push yourself, and you might go nowhere.

The timeline will depend on the type of project you're writing and why you're writing it.

A short e-book to sell on Amazon is generally 15,000–30,000 words (about 60–120 traditional pages). This type of book is a fantastic way to build your business or share your message. Projects like these are trending now, and for good reason. If you have a small business (maybe you're a consultant, coach, or service provider), people like to get a taste of what you'd be like to work with. (Maybe that's why you bought this book; you were curious what type of advice I offer as a writing coach). If you sell a product, your short e-book can offer more information about how to use your product. If you write on a broad topic, you can split the topic into a series of smaller e-books, rather than one massive tome.

A full-length manuscript tends to be 60,000–80,000 words (or 240–320 pages). Really, anything more than 80,000 words is massive and should either be split into several books or cut down significantly. This is traditional book length, like you are used to seeing on the shelves of Barnes and Noble. Some people do read these longer books on their e-readers. (I do, for one). But many don't have the patience to read all the way through a long book on a device. You may consider printing this length of book to sell as a paperback, as well as publishing on an e-platform.

So, think about what type of book you're writing, and pick a goal word count. Let's use the assumption that you're writing a long e-book of 25,000 words. That was my goal for this book.

Then, decide how many words per week

you're going to try to write. As we talked about in the previous section, 5,000 per week is a good clip.

So, 5,000 words per week for a 25,000-word e-book makes five weeks. But I'm going to ask you to do some free-writing too. Plus, you should include just a little extra wiggle room for your first book. (Unless you're working with a writing coach, then you'll be sure to stick to your schedule.) I'd suggest seven weeks is a great timeline for completing a first draft.

Here's what you would write out for yourself:

"I will write my 25,000-word e-book in seven weeks, at a pace of 5,000 words per week."

Put that in writing. Schedule it in your calendar. I literally pull up my Google calendar and my paper planner, and I mark out "Week 1," "Week 2," all the way through "Week 7" so that I can see how much time I have. Make it visual.

Then, plan out how often and for what length of time you'll try to write. Again, this is a best-guess, because you may not know at what pace you write. To start with, I suggest plugging in five hours of writing into your calendar for the week.

I know I'm a fast writer, so I aim for three. For me, this looks like 30 minutes every weekday and one more 30-minute chunk on the weekend. I don't get super-crazy about this. If it's 25 minutes one session, that's fine. If I miss a weekday session, that's fine, I just double up on the weekend. These are guidelines. Try to hit them, but don't beat yourself up if you don't.

Also note, I don't always write six times per week. This is when I'm actively writing a long project, like a book. Writing occurs in seasons. During a "normal" season, I write maybe 15 minutes each day, just free-writing, plus whatever writing time I need for my blog posts. During "high" season, like book-writing season, I try to stay devoted to writing for three hours per week, 5,000 words per week. Everyone can stick this out for a few months. It's not that hard! Certainly not that hard when the reward for your three to five hours per week is a book!

Next, we're ready to start real writing. It's all well and good to guess about word counts and timelines and writing sessions. Now we're ready to sit down at the computer and write. Are you ready?

Free-write on the topic

I recommend that you spend the first full week of writing doing free-writing exercises, which we covered in the last chapter on good writing habits. Most authors have been thinking about a book for long enough that they have a lot more ideas floating in their heads than words down on paper. The trouble is it's difficult to examine, organize, and clarify ideas in your head. You need them in actual words. After a week of free-writing, you'll probably have 5,000 to 10,000 words, maybe more if you're a very quick typist. The free-writing will be fodder for the rough organization of your book.

Draft the rough organization

During the second week of writing, you'll be planning a rough organization of your book. You can skim back through your free-writing, if you want. Often, though, you may find that simply having typed out your thoughts helps you organize them. You may feel clear enough just to sit down on Week 2, Day 1 and start typing out a rough draft organization of your book.

When creating a rough draft of your organization, don't feel bound to any particular method. If a mind-map or outline works for you, that's fine, but I haven't worked with a lot of clients who find those tools useful. Mind-maps tend to get unwieldy and confusing quickly. Outlines tend to stifle your creative flow.

What I recommend is a rough list, grouped into sections, and by rough, I do mean rough. Let me give you a sample of how I wrote the organization for this book:

MYTHS AND TRUTHS OF BECOMING A SUCCESSFUL AUTHOR

Myths that writers buy into.

You have to be someone special to be a successful writer (talented).

You have to have a lot of free time.

You have to write every day.

You need connections (agents, publishers).

You will probably spend a lot of money (some, not a lot).

If you're successful, you'll make a ton of money.

Truths:

Anyone can be a writer. It's more about persistence than talent.

Writing can be done in 5 hours a week.

Consistently, preferably according to a schedule, but not every day.

You don't need connections, but you do need to be willing to go out and talk to people.

You will spend some money (editors, proofreaders, formatters, designers).

Sorry, for most people, even successful authors, the book is not about money, it's about influence.

WHY WRITE A BOOK

There are a lot of good reasons to write a book.

You feel a mysterious call/curiosity.

You have some knowledge, advice, or experience that you'd like to share.

You have a story that would help others.

You have a business, and you want to be perceived as an expert. (Every field has experts. If not you, it will probably be someone less worthy.)

You want to start a business.

You have a message that you want to get out through every way possible—blog, podcast, YouTube, speaking gigs—and a book is part of that message platform.

HOW TO PREVENT SELF-SABOTAGE

I can promise that you will try to talk yourself out of writing your book nearly every writing session, if not every writing session. You'll begin to hear voices. Those voices of negativity have always been with you, but there's something about writing that releases them from their cages. How to not listen to them.

Stay connected with your WHY.

Recruit at least one person who will support you unconditionally.

Recruit at least one person who will read your writing and give you thoughtful, constructive challenges.

Commit to writing 5,000 words per week, even if you have to tell yourself that you're just brainstorming and no one will ever read those words.

Start thinking of yourself as a writer, allow it to become part of your identity.

Read books that encourage writing (like this one,

and a list of my favorite books by authors).

Listen to podcasts about writing.

Add: fear that people will judge your message/philosophy/voice—assume you're speaking to a supportive audience.

GOOD WRITING HABITS

Write only on one or two devices. I've had clients who have four, five, or six different desktops/laptops/phones/tablets for writing. Keeping all of those places synced is nearly impossible, even with cloud technology. You're still playing with too many platforms and asking for trouble.

Pick a writing software and stick with it. Word works just fine for most people. Google Docs, Scrivener, Evernote. If you're intrigued, here are some links. I use Scrivener. Mostly, though, the software isn't nearly as important as your commitment to steady progress. Write by hand. Speak into a recorder. Hire someone to convert those to digital word formats.

Free-writing.

Pomodoro.

Small chunks. I DO NOT recommend devoting an entire day or weekend or week just to writing. It's not a productive use of time. You'll probably get, at most, four hours of writing done in a day. When you're relaxed, thinking that you have all the time in the world, guess what, you take all the time in the world. THE EXCEPTION: You're almost done with your draft, your deadline is looming, and you have some adrenaline behind you.

Parkinson's Law: work expands so as to fit the time available for its completion. Use to your advantage.

Commit to 5,000 words per week.

Or commit to writing one sentence per day.

Some people say to leave off mid-thought or mid-sentence. That would drive me crazy. I'd be paranoid that I'd forget the thought! I complete my thoughts, and then I leave at least one area/point that I'd like to explore in my next writing session, just so I don't sit down to a blank screen.

Excel spreadsheet/calendar/track record.

Talk about your book with someone at least once a month, no more than once a week. (More than once a week, and you run the risk of becoming too narcissistic and self-reflective about your writing. There's a fine balance between talking/thinking about writing and actually writing.)

Carry a notebook or have some way to capture ideas on the fly. I like Evernote on my phone, personally.

And I would show you the rest, but that would spoil the book!

I have the sections in all caps and just a list of ideas in each section. You can see that I'm somewhat listing, somewhat writing notes to myself. It doesn't need to be perfect, as long as you remember what you want to say about each point in each topic.

You'll notice that this draft of the rough organization of this book doesn't match this published version that you're reading now. That's fine and, really, to be expected. Your chapters will change and shift a bit with each draft.

In the rough organization, you can also consider adding notes where you'll need to include research. This particular book is not research-heavy because it's based on my own experience as a writing coach. But many nonfiction books do include a lot of research. Come up with your own system. Maybe inserting a [*note] would indicate where you'll need to reference a study. Then, you could always run a search in the document for the * symbol to double-check that you included the research.

I don't want you to get sidetracked by the research, though. Only include research you need to support your main argument. Get your main argument down first, then the research. (Besides, if you're like most nonfiction writers, you have more research in your brain than is really useful.) It's time to stop focusing on research for a little while and focus on your own words. You'll be able to add layers of research in the second and subsequent drafts.

It may take you a few writing sessions to flesh out the rough organization, but not more than a week's worth of writing sessions. By the end of Week 2, you should have a good idea of what you're writing about.

Write the first draft

Before you launch in to the first draft, there is an option at this point. You can write a book proposal first. If you're planning to submit a proposal to a publisher, now is the time to start writing it. I've included helpful resources for writing a book proposal in Appendix A. If you're not submitting to a publisher, though, you don't have to write a proposal. You can move right on through to writing the first draft.

If you're planning to self-publish, Weeks 3–7 should be dedicated to the first draft.

Here's how I write my first drafts in Scrivener, which is the software that is becoming increasingly popular with writers. (Although, remember, specialty software does not a successful author make.)

I open a new project. I create a folder for my free-writings and copy/paste those in. I create a new note for my rough organization. I use the "Manuscript" section and start adding new notes, each with the title of the section/chapter. I split the screen vertically. In the top half, I am looking at the rough organization. In the bottom half, I am looking at the chapter that I'm currently writing. And I just follow the rough organization straight down, elaborating and explaining in the chapter itself.

You can do something similar in Word. You can have one document for your whole manuscript. The first five or so pages would be your rough organization, and the rest of the document would be your draft. You could split the screen, keeping the rough organization in one half, and typing the draft in the other half of the screen.

Your *only* goal at this point is to write all the way through the first draft. You write without editing. You write without hardly looking back at what you've written (only to remember where you left off in the last session). You keep pressing forward.

This will be a huge challenge. One that's near-insurmountable for many writers. Writing the first draft is like being in the Fire Swamp in *The Princess Bride*. There are dangers all around—eruptions of fire, rodents of unusual size, and dreaded quicksand. Looking back on your work to edit or even just to read is to step into quicksand. You'll sink and never resurface.

Don't look back. Keep writing.

As Will Self says, "Don't look back until you've written an entire draft, just begin each day from the last sentence you wrote the preceding day.

This prevents those cringing feelings, and means that you have a substantial body of work before you get down to the real work which is all in ... the edit."[15]

Like Will, I recommend writing straight through the draft, from the first point in your rough organization to the last. I know that some people recommend writing with what's easiest or skipping around to different chapters, depending on what inspires you that day. I think that technique makes it too easy to get lost in what you were talking about and, ultimately, lose motivation in the project. When you work straight through, you know how much progress you're making in the book—which is exciting and urges you forward—and you're more likely to maintain a logical, coherent flow from one point to the next because that's exactly how you wrote it.

Remember, though, this is merely the process I recommend. If you start writing straight through and get stuck, tweak the system to work for you. Skip a chapter, if you have to. Just make sure to be extra attentive when you reach the revision stage.

As you're writing, you'll inevitably come up with a point that you need to reference, and you'll want to drop everything to Google a source or drive to the library to research the slightest detail. Even in this book, when I was writing the first draft of this section, I couldn't remember what the

---

15 Self, Will. "Ten rules for writing fiction (part two)," *The Guardian*, 20 February 2010.

swamp in *The Princess Bride* was called. As much as I wanted to stop writing and pull up Google to look up the name of the swamp, I reined myself in. Instead, I reminded myself that my priority was to keep writing the draft, so I made a note to myself to research the name of the swamp later.

I literally typed in: "Writing the first draft is like being in the [*Princess Bride Swamp]." Later, I searched my document for *, Googled the reference, and filled in the gap with "Fire Swamp." At all costs, try to avoid interrupting your writing flow with Google searches, digging through your digital database of research, or even looking in a thesaurus. You just want to stay in the flow of writing. Make * notes of anything that would require you to leave the writing window.

That said, there are some occasions when you do need to pause writing to research something. Maybe the point is especially relevant to a chapter you're writing, and you need a refresher on what the research says. Maybe you're legitimately looking for inspiration or to see whether any new research has popped up since you last looked. There are two ways to approach research time while writing—one for quick lookups of research that you already know exists, and one for more in-depth research to add to the argument of your book. We'll take them one at a time.

First, for quicker, scanning research, make a list of the points you need to research, and use the Pomodoro technique. Set a timer for 25 minutes. Start with the highest priority research topic, and focus only on that while the timer is running. You're trying to be hyper-focused, so that you can find what you need to know for the book and move on. Don't be tempted to dive down the rabbit hole of research. Don't feel like you need to be the best-informed expert on this topic in order to write about it.

For every topic, there is an overwhelming amount of research available, whether you're writing about growing a sustainable garden or the neuroscience of speech, there will be volumes and volumes of digital data. It would take you *years* to comb through it all. Maybe you already have spent years, and you've delayed writing your book because you feel the need to research more.

Ultimately, your addiction to research is a manifestation of your own self-doubt. You don't feel smart enough, worthy enough, or informed enough to write on your topic. You're convinced that, if you just borrow the intelligence, worthiness, and information from other people, your book will have some value. But then, and only then, do you think you'll feel worthy.

But I want you to know that you *already* have enough information and research to write your book. Sure, okay, it's not going to be the ultimate book that combines every single bit of research that's ever been done. One book isn't supposed to do that, though. This book can be the first of many books you write on your subject. And maybe after a few books, you'll start to feel increasingly like an expert in the field.

You don't have to be the ultimate expert before you start writing a book because the process of writing a book is a journey toward expertise. You have enough to start writing your book, with perhaps small, timed pauses for research.

As much as I would caution you to not fall into the trap of thinking that you already have to be an expert on a topic before writing a book, there's also the truth that some topics simply require more research than others. When you find that you honestly do need to do more in-depth research and review the existing literature in order to add a new chapter or strengthen an argument, there is a method that will keep you writing as you go.

Use the Pomodoro method here, as well. Make a list of the points you need to research, even if it's only categories or author names or theories. The more specific you can be, the more focused you'll remain. Read in 25-minute chunks, with 5-minute breaks between. If you're diving deep into lengthy articles and books, it will be tempting to read straight through for hours, but your brain needs to process in chunks in order to remember the information and apply it to the book you're writing.

For every two to three 25-minute chunks of reading you do, commit one 25-minute chunk of time just for writing your reflections on the research. You can write notes, free-write, or journal. Just make sure that you're writing a response to what you're reading in your own words.

I can't emphasize enough how critical it is to continue writing while researching. Many people think that when they get writer's block, they can simply go look for inspirational material and read until they feel like writing again. Inevitably, they read hundreds of pages of material and yet don't feel any more inspired to return to their writing project. If anything, they feel an even *more* urgent need to research further. Research is addictive. The more you research, the more you'll feel an adrenaline kick and the refrain begins to echo in your mind, "I need to learn more. There's so much I don't know. I need to become an expert. And there's so much more I'll have to read in order to become one."

There it is—that feeling you that you must read *everything* in order to be worthy to write this book. It's simply not true. Even if you're writing on a research-heavy topic, you probably have already done quite a lot of reading on the topic. Read what you can, write as you read, and push yourself to continue on through the first draft.

If you need to break from writing for a period of in-depth research, I recommend limiting yourself to no more than a week at a time. What does this look like? You'll have written out your timeline, done your free-writing for a week, drafted a rough organization, and maybe written on your first draft for a week before you realize you need some in-depth research time.

Take a week, max, to do Pomodoro-style

research, making sure to write your reflections in between. After one week of research, force yourself back into writing the first draft, continuing to follow the rough organization. Don't allow yourself to fall into the black hole of endless research. One week is plenty, then continue writing the draft. You can always add a week of research here and there throughout the writing process, but every week that you spend researching is another week added on to how long it will take you to finish your first draft.

As you write your first draft, you'll encounter resistance. Steven Pressfield has written a brief but remarkably powerful book on resistance and being an artist (which includes writing) in his book, *The War of Art*. Pressfield says, "Most of us have two lives. The life we live, and the unlived life within us. Between the two stands Resistance."[16] Resistance is that impersonal force that makes it difficult for you to succeed at changing something in your life. The change you're working on now is becoming an author. You will feel *a lot* of resistance at various points of writing your first draft.

People feel resistance to start writing. In many writers, the resistance manifests itself in reading a lot of books about writing without doing any actual writing, prioritizing cleaning the house over writing, talking to friends about writing but not

---

[16] Pressfield, Steven. *The War of Art: Break Through the Blocks and Win Your Inner Creative Battles*. 2012. Black Irish Entertainment, LLC: New York, NY.

making time to write, and claiming you're too busy to write. Sometimes people get physically ill or have a slew of home improvement problems just when they think they're ready to start writing.

People often feel resistance when they're partway through their first draft. They re-read what they've written, over and over again. They edit what they've written, trying to make it perfect as they go. They write a bit and then have months of "research" time, during which they're not actively reading or writing. They have a slump week (or month) without a lot of writing and aren't able to find their momentum again. They have recurring thoughts like, "This book isn't original," "I'm not smart/talented/creative enough to write this book," "I'm just not a good writer," or "No one is going to want to read this." Those are all resistance at its finest.

All writers feel resistance after they've finished their first draft. They congratulate themselves on a job accomplished and never revisit the manuscript. It lies on the hard drive, gathering digital dust. They're too self-conscious to read back through the manuscript, worried that they're going to finally find out that they're a terrible writer and all-around not worth a reader's attention.

This resistance is universal. Every single author has struggled with all of these thoughts.

Tennessee Williams had the guts to say what every successful author has thought, "I don't believe anyone ever suspects how completely unsure I am of my work and myself and what tortures of self-doubting the doubt of others has always given me."[17]

But you must find a way to cope with resistance and self-doubt. Go back to the chapter on preventing self-sabotage, and re-read it. Remind yourself why this book is important to you. Practice free-writing, even when you don't feel like writing. Call up your accountability partner and admit that you're in a slump. The resistance will not go away on its own. Embrace the resistance as a natural part of the writing process. Forgive yourself, and simply press on. Writing will not get easier, but you will get used to recognizing resistance when you feel it, and learn how to cope.

Write the introduction and title

I prefer to write the introduction and come up with the book title after the rest of the first draft is complete. To me, it makes sense to introduce and title something that has already been written.

After you have written all the way through your rough organization, go back to the beginning and draft your introduction. Write in one to five paragraphs why this book is important to the reader. Identify the problem that the reader is having (or the problem that exists in the world), how your book offers a solution or additional insight, and how the reader (or the world) will

---

[17] Williams, Tennessee. *The Selected Letters of Tennessee Williams: 1920–1945*. 2000. New Directions Publishing: New York, NY.

experience some transformation because of your book. Then, you can brainstorm titles.

Congratulations! You have finished your first draft. It won't be perfect. You probably won't even think it's that good. But you have a first draft, and that is an accomplishment to be acknowledged. Be proud of yourself and take at least a day to celebrate.

The next chapter, on revising the draft, will walk you through revisions and getting feedback from an editor and beta readers. What you do after the first draft, that's what will make an author out of you.

CHAPTER FIVE

Beyond the first draft

I would love to tell you that after writing the first draft, the hardest part is over. I'm sorry, but getting through the first draft is easy compared to what's to follow. Writing the first draft is a beautiful time because you have so many fresh ideas, bursts of creative insights, and ah-ha moments. And you're not editing, just writing straight through.

Now, it's time to revise. This is when the writer turns into an author. This is when the hobbyist turns into a professional. If you can revise a draft, you are in exceptional company. It doesn't take any special talent to revise a draft—just a nearly inhuman amount of patience and persistence. This is your book, though, and it's worth every ounce of determination you have in order to make it the best book it can be.

Those demons that reared their ugly heads while you were writing your first draft? You may have hushed them up long enough to finish the draft, but they'll be back stronger than ever as you enter the revision phase. You'll read back over what you've written and feel a whole new slew of negative thoughts rise up: "How could I think this is good?" "It doesn't even make sense!" "What was I thinking?" "I don't have a clue how to organize all of this crap." Or, even worse: "Meh, I don't feel like revising. This is good enough as is."

When you hear the reverberation of negative thoughts in your head, don't panic. Just return to the chapter on preventing self-sabotage and refresh your spirit. Talk to yourself on a daily basis about why this book is important to you and to the reader. When you can't muster the strength to revise, free-write about the resistance you're feeling. Lean on your accountability partner. Know that the resistance will always be there, but maintain your commitment to press on.

Steel yourself. Know that you're not alone. This chapter is here to guide you step-by-step through the revision process in a simple, straightforward, logical way that will help you edit with confidence, knowing that you're revising the sections that are weakest and strengthening the sections that are already powerful and clear.

I recommend that you do not start with page 1 and read through the whole draft all over again, trying to edit as you go. You'll be completely discouraged by page 10, confused by page 45, and you'll have stopped caring by page 70.

Instead, I suggest following a revision process, which will look something like this:

- Initial read-through and reverse outline (2–4 days)
- First revision (1 week)
- Send to editor (2–3 weeks)*
- Second revision (1 week)
- Send to beta readers (2–3 weeks)**
- Third revision (1–2 days)
- Proofread (1–2 days)
- Read aloud (1–2 days)

* If you are planning to bring in a professional editor, I recommend doing the reverse outline and first edit before handing off the manuscript. You'll have done just enough editing that the editor will have a good idea of what the structure of the book will look like, but you won't have done so much editing that you're emotionally attached to everything that's in the manuscript.

** You can switch whether you send to beta readers first or the editor first, depending on your timeline and your editor's availability.

Initial read-through and reverse outline

First, try to emotionally distance yourself from your manuscript. When you pull up the file with your first draft, take a moment to remind yourself that these are simply words on a page. These words do not reflect your self-worth. These words will not be perfect. At times, they will not make sense or will sound just wrong. They are only words. Words are moveable, flexible, changeable. You wrote the words, yes, but now you will rearrange, delete, and add more words to try to get at a clearer message.

There will be carving and cutting, and it will feel painful at times, but the amount of revisions your manuscript requires says nothing about you as a writer. Your willingness to chop up your first draft in order to better serve your readership, though, that says everything about you as a writer. Don't focus on your own worthiness as a writer; focus on how you can best encourage and inspire your audience.

Now you are ready for the initial read-through of your manuscript. Read quickly, not stopping to change anything and not dwelling on how to word a concept. While reading, you'll be taking notes. You can take notes by hand, with a notebook and pen (my preferred method), or a stack of note cards, or you can open up a document side-by-side, sharing the screen with your manuscript.

As you read, you'll be creating a reverse

outline. This is, essentially, a traditional outline, but you're creating the outline as you read. Write down the chapter title. As you read each paragraph, create a sub-point in the outline that summarizes the paragraph in one sentence or phrase. With every paragraph that you read, write down a sub-point underneath the main header.

When you're finished, you should have an outline that accurately reflects the point that each paragraph is making, in the order that the points are presented in the draft.

Once you've finished the reverse outline, you'll be able to rethink your structure. Looking at a reverse outline of your draft is like maintaining a bird's-eye view of the main points in your book. Now you can delete, rearrange, and add to those points. Make notes in the reverse outline itself. Maybe you'll want to move one paragraph up because it fits more naturally with the three paragraphs at the beginning of the section. Maybe you'll want to delete a paragraph, because it repeats the point from a previous paragraph, or combine the two paragraphs. Maybe you'll notice a paragraph that makes an important point but is very short, so you'll want to add content to clarify there.

As you notice what you want to change, make notes. Try comment bubbles in your reverse outline document, sticky notes on an actual paper version of the reverse outline, or write in a different color—whatever works for your system.

Important! We are only adjusting the

structure of the manuscript here, which means that we're staying at paragraph-level. We're not adjusting individual sentences, wording, or even spelling. Ignore all of that. If you get sucked into looking at details, you will not be able to maintain a broad overview of the manuscript.

(I've included an example of a reverse outline of this book in Appendix C. I've also included a bonus worksheet, with some guided questions to help you as you create your own reverse outline.)

With the reverse outline of your first draft in hand, you have a roadmap for your revisions. You'll feel confident that you're making the right adjustments to the draft because you'll know how the entire manuscript looks now and how you want it to look when you're finished with revisions.

Take a break, preferably for at least a day. When you're refreshed, you'll be ready for the first revision.

First revision

Go back to page one. Now you're ready to edit from the first page to the last. Keep your reverse outline next to you as you go through, paragraph by paragraph. Refer to your notes in the reverse outline about which paragraphs needed adjusting, deleting, combining, or clarifying. Make sure your sentences are concise, not repetitive, and necessary to make the point that is relevant to the paragraph.

The first edit can be a little overwhelming because you're looking at more than one aspect of the manuscript at a time. 1) The broad structure. Referring constantly to your reverse outline, you are making adjustments to each paragraph, to make sure the points logically progress from one paragraph to the next and that they build on each other to support your book's main argument. 2) Sentence structure. You want to make sure that each sentence is worded in a powerful, clear way to best deliver your message.

Armed with your annotated reverse outline, you should be ready to tackle the broad structure, so let's talk about sentence structure and some of the most common sentence-level mistakes that authors make while writing the first draft.

- Sentence length
- Sentence variety
- Repetition and vagueness
- Word choice
- Acronyms

Sentence length

If you're not paying attention, you run the risk of writing sentences that are all the same length. Sentences tend to range from 10 to 40 words, and individuals often write sentences on one end of the spectrum or the other.

To figure out whether you have a tendency toward writing shorter or longer sentences, pull out three paragraphs of your first draft and count the number of words in each sentence. For example, I went back to the beginning of this chapter and pulled the first three paragraphs. Here are my word counts for each sentence: 17 – 15 – 22 – 9 – 5 – 9 – 9 – 11 – 19 – 25 – 14 – 25 – 46 – 15

You can see that my sentences vary from short (5, 9, 11 words) to mid-length (19, 22, 25). I only have one especially long sentence at the end there. Of course, I'm cheating a bit because those word counts are from a revised version of those sentences. In my natural state, I write very long sentences (easily 30–40 words), so I make a conscious effort to chop my sentences in half during my revision process.

The problem with long sentences of 30+ words is that they require the reader to hold several concepts and how they relate to each other in their minds for a long time. Hitting the reader with wave after wave of long sentences, and a series of clauses and phrases strung together, never letting the reader take a break, and then adding a conjunction, just to make the sentence longer, leaves the reader gasping for air by the time he reaches the period. And that last sentence was only 50 words. Imagine reading three or four of those long sentences in a row! It's exhausting for the reader.

Even if your reader is very smart and perfectly capable of holding multiple concepts in her mind at once, long sentences are not necessarily the best way to communicate. Most readers simply don't want to drag their way through long sentences. And why would you, the writer, ask them to? Your goal is to guide the reader through your ideas so that she understands them. The key word here is "guide," not "drag" the reader through long, windy sentences that bore him to death. If you find yourself writing sentences that are 40+ words long or frequently using conjunctions ("and," "but," "yet"), go back and see if you can break up some of those sentences.

Short sentences can be problematic, too. When the reader processes too many short sentences back-to-back, he'll become frustrated because he encounters the same concept from one sentence to the next, and the choppy flow makes it difficult to integrate new information about the concept across sentences. Let me give you an example. (I made these up, so the "results" are completely fictional.)

"I ran a regression model on two variables, education and income. The data showed that education has a positive correlation with income. The results indicate that with each increased level of education, income increases an average of $20,000."

The first sentence is 11 words, the second is also 11, and the third is 16. Try reading all three of the sentences aloud. Do you hear the choppiness? There's no good rhythm from one sentence to the next. When periods interrupt the flow so frequently, it's difficult for the reader to find the connection between the concepts and integrate the information into one, cohesive picture. Each sentence requires the reader to start over trying to understand the objects (variables, education and income, increased level) and how they relate to each other.

Now try this one sentence:

"I ran a regression model on education and income, which showed that not only were the two variables positively correlated, but with each increased level of education, income increased an average of $20,000."

Since it's one sentence, the reader knows that the concepts addressed by the sentence are education and income, and with each phrase the reader encounters in the sentence, he integrates the new information smoothly and easily. If you tend toward very short sentences, you can increase the effectiveness of your communication by finding two sentences that are very closely related and combining them.

I'm not suggesting that every one of your sentences should be 25–35 words long. You'll need a variety of sentences, depending on what you're trying to communicate in that moment. If you're trying to explain the relationship between two concepts, you may opt for a longer sentence. If you want to drive an important point home, short sentences are often very powerful. The best writing intentionally uses a variety of sentences.

Mostly, what I would encourage you to do is to start paying attention. You probably already have a pretty good idea of which sections in your writing have too many short or long sentences; it's just that you don't usually bother going back to revise them.

Simply trying to avoid one extreme or another will certainly help you improve your writing.

Sentence variety

When you're in a good writing groove during the first draft phase, those days when you may easily churn out several thousand words, that's when you're probably writing formulaic sentences. It's completely unintentional, but when you feel totally at ease and in the flow of writing, you're probably relying on habits you've established over the years of writing, maybe even from grade school.

Maybe you tend to start sentences with "while" or "although," so that every other sentence has a structure that looks like this: "While x seems to be true, y is actually true."

Maybe you tend to list things in groups of three. (I do this!). You end every paragraph with a trio of helpful points, great tips, and clever tricks.

Or is it possible that you ask a lot of rhetorical questions, rather than simply stating your point?

I'm poking fun, but sentence variety is a serious matter. When you're going through the manuscript during your first edit, you'll need to be on the lookout for habits you've developed in structuring your sentences.

Repetition and vagueness

When you're writing the first draft, you're trying to get clear in your own mind how you want to explain something. Some writers tend toward over-explaining, some toward under-explaining.

Over-explaining manifests itself in repetition. With your reverse outline next to you, you can look at a specific paragraph, see what you wrote down as the summary, and then examine each sentence within that paragraph to see how it relates to that summary. Sometimes you make a point in the first sentence of the paragraph, then the next two or three sentences are just repeated variations of that first sentence. That will annoy your reader, who we must assume is fairly intelligent and will understand your point after only being told once. Look for places where you can delete repetitive phrases, combine sentences, and cut sentences entirely (which often means you may combine two paragraphs).

Under-explaining is equally annoying to a reader. Usually, when your writing is described as "vague," it means you're not taking the time to fully articulate your point. Each paragraph should have one summary point. If you find that you write paragraphs that have two or more summary points, then you're probably cramming too many arguments into a short space, which is only possible if you're not explaining each argument well.

Look for paragraphs that are very short (only one or two sentences) and paragraphs that contain two or more summary points. You can probably add sentences to elaborate on your point and build out paragraphs with added explanations.

Word choice

Some authors tend toward very natural, casual language, which is great for connecting with the reader, but tends to use a lot of the same words, over and over. Other authors are intentional about how often they use a word and will rely heavily on a thesaurus to bring in word choice variety, which is great for higher-level prose but can unnecessarily alienate even the smartest of readers.

Casual word choice is in vogue right now. Basically, every editor, writing coach, and copywriter will tell you to write the way you speak, for a lot of good reasons. Writing the way you speak allows readers to connect more immediately with what you're trying to say, forces you to explain difficult concepts in everyday language, and makes you come across like a human being. The issue is we're narrow in our vocabulary when speaking. This doesn't bother us when we're in verbal conversations, but in written prose, it'll drive the reader crazy.

As you read, keep an eye out for your go-to words. Keep a running list (I use a "Sticky" on my Mac), and as you're editing, run searches for your commonly used words. Replace them when it feels like there's a natural synonym. Use thesaurus.com—my favorite free writing tool.

If you tend toward the other end of the spectrum, with more formal language, then your prose could probably use an injection of approachability. If you don't even blink at words that end in "-tion" like, "gentrification," "radicalization," or "feminization," then you probably have a high tolerance for alienating words. Even if you're writing for academic audiences, you'll make more of an impact on your reader if you tone down the formality of your language. You can explain even very complex concepts with common words.

Look for jargon, words that end in "-tion," and anything you might find on a college entrance exam prep list. Consider whether that's the best word to use or whether there's another, simpler way to talk about the concept. I'm not saying to dumb down your language. I'm suggesting that you become more intentional about your words and don't just rely on the heavy jargon language just because it comes more easily to you.

Acronyms

Overuse of acronyms will frustrate your reader, too. If you've been researching a topic for months or years, it may feel natural to use acronyms throughout your book. However, it's quite likely your reader will forget what the acronym stands for after the third reference and then be annoyed every time you use it.

Either find alternative ways to reference the

acronym or remind your reader on a regular basis (at a minimum every chapter) what the acronym stands for. I definitely understand that if you're writing about anything to do with the government—let's say U.S. education—it's really tempting to use NCLB for No Child Left Behind, PD for Professional Development, and SASS for the Schools and Staffing Survey throughout your manuscript. Sure, 25% of your readers may be experts like yourself and catch onto all the acronyms, because they spend their spare time reading about the same programs and departments that you do. If you want to broaden the impact of your book, though, you need to make it more accessible. Acronyms are one of the most frustrating yet easily fixed word choices in nonfiction writing.

Do yourself and your reader a favor—be very careful and intentional around your use of acronyms.

Consistency by creating a style sheet

A style sheet is a set of "rules" that are unique to your piece of writing. It tracks all the spelling, capitalization, and stylistic decisions you make for your book. As you edit your first draft, have a blank document or sheet of paper, and every time you come across a particular choice you've made (maybe you decide to use "U.S." rather than "US", for instance), write it down on your style sheet. This will be critical for the proofreading stage. You'll refer back to this style sheet to make sure that all of your choices are consistent throughout your book.

Editor

I recommend involving an editor before bringing in your beta readers. This is personal preference and somewhat dependent on your timeline and the editor's availability. I think of my beta readers as my target audience. I want to give them as clean a version of the book as possible, so that their feedback is focused. An editor can see through the typos and grammar errors to get to the core of the book, but beta readers will get easily tripped up on superficial problems. If you're pressed for time and your editor isn't available for another month, feel free to pull in beta readers early, so long as you warn them not to get hung up on typos and grammar errors.

Finding the right editor is like any other service. Personality matters. Find someone who clicks with you and your project. Your working relationship is important. If you're the type of person who focuses only on price, then you'll probably have a less-than-ideal relationship with your editor, because editors who hire out for $15/hour will likely have so many clients that they can't forge true relationships with their writers.

I believe that the relationship between writer and editor is critical for producing a quality book. For that reason, I look for editors that meet a few of my own personal requirements:

- A website and blog. I want to know what they're writing about and how they talk to potential clients. You can find out a lot about an editor from her website.

- An easy-to-understand pricing model. I like per word or per package pricing. I think roughly four cents per word is very reasonable for high-quality editing.

- Responsive to email. When I send a query asking for when the editor will be available, I expect a response within three business days. Otherwise, she's too busy for my project.

- Willing to give references. If I ask for references, she should be able to provide two references for projects similar to mine.

- A personality that I jive with. I'm fairly easy-going and casual, but I also like responsiveness and promptness, so I look for similar qualities in my editor.

Ultimately, you just have to go with your gut and hire someone. If it doesn't work out, you can always find someone else. You can look at upwork.com, but your best editors aren't on upwork.com or any other freelance website because they have their own platforms for reaching clients. I prefer to Google a variety of search terms ("book editing," "freelance editing," nonfiction editing," "nonfiction e-book editing," and various combinations). I also ask my Facebook and private communities for suggestions.

My strong recommendation is that you contact a couple of editors when you're still writing your first draft. Good editors book out anywhere from two weeks to six months in advance, depending on their business model. As soon as you can, get in touch with an editor and start lining up a timeframe for when you'll send her the manuscript, how long it'll take her to return it, and what her follow-up process is for an additional editing passes.

For instance, with my clients, I always do two editing passes. The client sends me the manuscript. I edit once and send it back to him. He makes last changes and sends it back to me. Then, I line edit and proofread before sending it back the final time. My process requires at least 10 days of active back-and-forth. Schedule in some buffer time when you work with an editor.

Check in with your editor about two weeks before you're scheduled to finish your manuscript, just to make sure you're still on schedule. Authors are often flakey, so editors sometimes don't take seriously an author's promise of a draft ready by a certain date. But you're not that sort of author, right? You're on top of your game. I suggest sending a quick reminder email about two weeks out, saying, "Hey, just checking in. Are we still planning to start editing my book on May 14th? I'm on schedule to finish up the draft by May 10th, and I'll have it ready for you by the 14th." Something like that. Your editor should respond in a timely fashion.

When you send the manuscript, include a list of your concerns or questions about the manuscript. You can be as general or as specific as you like. Here are some example concerns and questions:

- I tend to write very long sentences. Can you help me break them up and make sure they're easily digestible for an average reader?
- I'm writing for an academic audience, so there's an expectation I'll use some jargon, but I don't want to be too obtuse. Could you help me find the balance between jargon that's useful for my audience and over-reliance on jargon?
- I'm having trouble putting together a compelling conclusion. Could you help me figure out a better way to tie everything together at the end?
- I know the manuscript slows down in the middle, but I'm not sure how to pick up the pace there. Could you let me know your thoughts about the pace of Chapters 3 and 4?

You get the idea. Feel free to share any concerns that you have about your manuscript so that your editor knows where to focus her attention. Of course, she'll be doing her best to root out every structural issue there is, but knowing what you're concerned about is extremely helpful.

Ask your editor when she hopes to turn the manuscript back around to you, and clear some space in your schedule to review the editor's changes as soon as possible. You want to make changes and ask any further questions fairly quickly after the editor returns the manuscript to you. Editors are like anyone else. They get busy and forget to follow up. It's in your best interest to be prepared to make changes and ask for any additional editing help you'll need.

This whole back-and-forth process with the editor should take two to three weeks, depending on the length of your manuscript and your editor's workflow. After you've gone through a second revision to incorporate the editor's suggestions, which might take another week, you're ready to involve your beta readers.

Beta readers

Now that your manuscript is at least clean enough to get feedback from readers, I recommend gathering a small group of beta readers, two to five people. Let everyone know ahead of time that you'd like their feedback. Give them a date when the manuscript will be ready for them to read—at least two weeks' notice is a good idea.

You definitely want to include your supporters and cheerleaders—your accountability partner and the people who asked about your book as you were writing. You may also want to ask someone who is more of an "expert," maybe someone who is a colleague, has published in the same field, or has some experience with writing. When you gather your two to five readers, let them know that they are your beta readers. Don't just say, "Hey, can you take a look at this?" Add a bit of seriousness to your request. This is an integral part of your book-writing process. Treat it as such.

Here's a checklist for interacting with your beta readers:

- Let them know ahead of time.
- Specify a deadline for feedback.
- Give them their own version of the document.
- Prepare specific questions for their feedback.
- Remind them a few days before the feedback deadline.
- Ask if they would mind reviewing the book on Amazon or Goodreads when it comes out.

- If they say yes, put them on a reviewer list for later.

Okay, so let's walk through all of those steps.

Let them know at least two weeks in advance when the manuscript will be ready and that you'll need feedback within two weeks of giving it to them. Never ask for feedback without a firm (but nicely worded) deadline. This is a serious work for you, and you need timely feedback.

How you send the manuscript and gather feedback is up to you. You can just email them a copy of the Word doc. (If you write in Scrivener, you'll have to export the file into Word. Scrivener isn't up to snuff with collaborative editing and version control.) Rename the Word doc so you don't get confused later. I use the same naming convention on all of my documents: "Title YY-MM-DD [Name]." When it's my version of a document, I would put "Title of My Book 15-04-08 [Morgan]." If I were sending it out to one of my beta readers on April 20, 2015, I would title her version of the document: "Title of My Book 15-04-20 [Darcy]." This just helps me keep track of when I gathered feedback and whose feedback it is.

When you send them the manuscript, instead of just saying, "Let me know what you think," ask for specific feedback. Prepare five to eight questions for the reviewer to answer. The best questions will depend on the book, but if you're really stuck, here's a sample of questions you could ask:

- What do you think of the premise of my book? (Provide a one-sentence summary, for example, "Do you think it's possible for someone to write a book, using the steps I outline in my book?")
- Were there any sections that you felt were slow or confusing?
- Were there any sections that were especially powerful or changed your perspective somehow?
- Is there anything that you would add to the book? Or any questions left unanswered?
- Was the overall tone approachable and likable to you?
- Where should I focus my revisions?
- Who do you think would enjoy or benefit most from this book?

After you send the manuscript and feedback questions to your beta readers, you can relax a bit. Maybe work on lining up your cover art and figure out how you're going to publish. This book is more about the writing process, but there are a lot of very helpful books on preparing for the publication process. (See Appendix A for more resources.)

Third revision, proofread, and read aloud

Go through a third revision to incorporate your beta readers' suggestions. Then, proofread your manuscript. I suggest reading the entire manuscript backward, from the last paragraph, all the way to the first. When you're reading a familiar piece of writing, your brain will skip over and correct mistakes on autopilot, so you won't even see them. Hyper-focus on each sentence at a time by reading backward, and you'll catch exponentially more errors. My final piece of advice is to read your entire book aloud. There is no better way to catch simple errors and typos. It's well worth the five-hour investment.

Before we finish up your book, let's take a few minutes to talk about how to handle criticism, because during this feedback process with your editor and beta readers, you'll receive a heck of a lot of feedback. It's easy (but oh-so-destructive) to take criticism the wrong way. Some simple suggestions can help you take it the right way and, as such, enhance your book beyond measure.

CHAPTER SIX

Dealing with criticism

Learning how to take criticism is one of the most vital steps to developing your craft as a writer. You can take all the seminars on writing you want, you can draft tens of thousands of words, but if you can't take feedback from a reader or editor and incorporate it into your manuscript, you'll sabotage your own writing success.

True, it's your manuscript, your book. So, it's your prerogative to decide whether to incorporate critical feedback or ignore it. However, you need to make sure you have the right attitude toward that feedback, so you're evaluating the criticism fairly. Here are three truths to help you put yourself in a mindset that's optimal for receiving and evaluating criticism:

- The person giving you feedback wants to help you make your book better. He has taken the time to read your book, created some responses to your book, and passed them along to you. All of this indicates that his underlying motive is to improve your book.

- There is some element of truth to the feedback. No matter how positive or negative the feedback is, there is some grain of truth to it, which means there is something that can be improved upon in your manuscript.

- *You are not your book.* Your value and worth as a person are not tied up in this book. If your reviewer says the book is terrible, it's no reflection on your worthiness as a person. By the same token, if the reviewer says the work is brilliant, that's no reflection on your worthiness either. The book is a crafted piece. Yes, you worked on it. Yes, you poured parts of yourself into it. But at the end of the day, your book could vanish into a black hole, yet you would still be a valuable, worthwhile, loved, and loving person. Separate yourself from your art in order to be fully open to criticism.

As you're about to encounter some form of feedback, whether it's in an email, an Amazon review, a phone call, or a meeting, remind yourself, "This person wants to help make my book better, there is some truth to what he has to say, and this feedback on my art does not diminish or enhance my value as a person." Psychology studies have shown that if you can focus on the big picture—that you want to be a better writer, that you want this book to be the best it can be—you'll be able to receive criticism without becoming defensive.[18]

Take a deep breath and open yourself up to the feedback, whether it's good or bad.

Be open to receiving criticism

Take in the criticism. You may be tempted to ignore the one-star review or not want to open the email that has your editor's feedback. You may push off meeting with one of your beta readers, who has some input for you. Stop procrastinating. Without this feedback, your book will stagnate. If you want to improve your book, you have to receive the feedback.

Collect and process the data

Maybe it's the social scientist in me, but I think of gathering feedback as a data collection process. I

[18] Belding, Jennifer N., Naufel, Karen Z., and Kentaro Fujita. "Using High-Level Construal and Perceptions of Changeability to Promote Self-Change Over Self-Protection Motives in Response to Negative Feedback." *Personality and Social Psychology Bulletin*. May 8, 2015.

ask for input from beta readers through email, phone, and face-to-face meetings. I prefer face-to-face meetings, but those can be intimidating. Two responses is an absolute minimum, but three to five would be ideal.

If you're receiving feedback through a phone or face-to-face meeting, take notes. Jot down the reader's main areas of concern. Make sure you fully understand the concern. Repeat it back to the person. If my beta reader, Elaine, is telling me that my book starts feeling slow or sluggish in the middle, I'll jot down "sluggish in the middle," and then repeat back to her, "So, it sounds like you're saying that the book was a little slower or less interesting after Chapter 7. Is that right?" I'll give her a chance to clarify, and then I'll ask follow-up questions: "Where did it start feeling slow to you?" "What is one part you would skip?" "Was there an exciting or especially interesting part before or after it was feeling slow?" Probe into the criticism; try to fully understand what is at the root of the criticism.

Often, readers don't even fully understand what it is that hits them wrong about a book. They'll say vague things like, "It was slow in the middle" or "It was confusing at parts," without pinpointing a particular place in the manuscript that was slow or confusing.

It's your job, as the author, to discover the underlying cause of their concern. You have to take down as many details as the reader is able to give you and then return to your manuscript, trying to identify anything that may have caused the reader's complaint.

If the reader simply says, "Chapter 3 felt a little slow to me," you should return to the end of Chapter 2 and read all the way through the beginning of Chapter 4 (targeting just before the problem area to just past the problem area) and look for anything that might cause a slower pace. Maybe longer sentences. Maybe too many personal stories. Maybe too much data. Maybe theoretical ideas with no concrete images or details. It could be any number of issues slowing the pace. Just because your reader doesn't identify exactly what caused the problem doesn't mean the problem isn't there.

It's not the reader's responsibility to know how to improve your book. It's yours.

After you've collected all of the email responses and notes from meetings, spread them all out in front of you. Look for patterns in the feedback. Are there particular sections in the book that people complain about? Is there a tendency in my style that hits people wrong? Are there any parts of my argument that people tend to disagree with? Is there a common sentiment of praise, something that everyone seems to like about the book?

Next, create a document that combines and summarizes the criticism. I use Excel, but you could certainly use a Word or Google Docs document or a paper notebook. Whatever feels most natural. Group common complaints and common praises together. Brainstorm ways to address them, and note where in the manuscript you think would be best to adjust.

Here's an example where the common complaint is that the book is "slow in the middle."

One column titled "Reviewer's input" would say, "Slow in the middle." List out the phrases that the reviewers used. "After about Chapter 4, you started to lose me. [Becky]" "I'm not sure exactly when it happened, but somewhere when you were talking about the editing process, it felt kind of sluggish. [Rob]" And so on.

The next column titled "My Responses" contains notes written to yourself. "I should check the word count of the chapters. It's definitely possible that the 'Beyond the first draft' chapter is just way too long. Maybe break it into chunks?"

The last column, "Where in the MS?" would indicate where in the manuscript (that's MS in the publishing world) you should implement changes. "'Beyond the first draft' chapter. Pages x–x."

Fill out the table with all of the reviewers' feedback. If there's something that you know you don't want to change, still include the feedback in the table, but your response in the table could be, "I don't want to change this because [whatever reason]." Any feedback that you don't act on should have a compelling reason. Don't ignore the criticism. Process it, either by adjusting something in the manuscript or by giving yourself a good reason why you're choosing to not change anything.

Underneath the table, feel free to also list a few positive remarks from the beta readers, to remind you of the good things that are already working in your draft. Remember that even when you're improving some parts of the draft, other parts are already good, powerful, and just fine the way they are.

(See Appendix C for an example and Bonus Worksheet on creating your own Feedback Table.)

Own your book

Remember, in the end, this is your book. Don't change anything that you truly don't want to change, even if every single reviewer complains about it. We don't like politicians who pander to the middle, and we don't like authors who tiptoe around, trying to make everyone happy. Just say what you want to say, the way you want to say it. Some will love your book, many will like it fine or feel relatively neutral, and some will absolutely hate it. This is true for every successful author. It'll be true for you, too.

CHAPTER SEVEN

Finished manuscript

When you finish your manuscript—first draft, revisions, and editor and beta readers' feedback incorporated—you have a completed book on your hands. Take a few minutes (or a few days) to celebrate! This is huge, seriously. More than 80% of Americans say they want to write a book someday,[19] but you have actually finished your book. You are among the elite, the few who persevere. Take some time to congratulate yourself.

You have to celebrate your milestones, because this is only one of many big steps along the path of getting your book out into the world. Writing the book is step one. Then, you'll need to

[19] Epstein, Joseph. Think You Have a Book in You? Think Again. *The New York Times,* September 28, 2002. NYTimes.com.

figure out design, marketing, and distribution.

Start Writing Your Book Today has walked you through the critical step of writing your book, but your time with me has come to an end. I'm no expert in formatting or marketing... yet! I'm learning myself, partly through my own release of this book. In Appendix A, I will leave you with some of the most helpful and up-to-date resources I've found in my own publishing path.

But my own journey in this digital publishing world is just beginning. And I hope you'll stay with me on this journey. I have visions of Google Hangouts, where we writers can gather online, read each other's drafts, and support each other through this grueling process of writing a book. I have plans for a book club, where together we read books on the craft of writing—Stephen King's *On Writing* and William Zinsser's *On Writing Well*—and we bounce ideas back and forth about how to improve our writing. I will soon be offering my own workshops and classes, online and in person, in the hopes of inspiring you and offering a helping hand as you write your book, wherever you are in the process or in the world.

If my vision resonates with you at all—if you love the idea of connecting with other writers and discussing books on writing craft—then let's connect.

Go to startwritingyourbooktoday.com, and let's get writing together!

— Morgan

Gratitude

I am overwhelmingly grateful for so many people in my life. My parents, Rhett and Janice: you have given me the foundational principles of my worldview—that God is good, that life is good—even amidst struggle—and that we are captains of our own destiny.

My siblings, Cutler, Kelson, and Darcy: you were the best inspiration when we were kids, and you're still my best friends. Darcy, especially, you're the best sister to do life with I could ever ask for.

My grandparents, Marie, Allen, Shirley, and Monty, and my aunt, uncles, and cousins, Darlene, Terry, Sarah, Mariah, and Marc: your belief in me to succeed has never wavered, and you remind me constantly how important family is to a good life. Thank you.

My husband, Chad: you push me to think about what is truly possible in life, and you support and love me unconditionally. My kiddos,

Cora, Ewan, and Meredith: you are my reasons for pursuing a life full of joy and purpose.

I have so many friends who have supported, loved, and encouraged me throughout the years. Heather, you found me eating lunch by myself in the library in seventh grade and made me become your friend, and you've always unreservedly told me that I'm a good writer. Kaycie, Katie, and Melissa: your lifelong friendship is such a security and comfort to me. Tara and Karen: you were with me as we all became purpose-driven adults, and you helped me grow into who I am today.

I have the best clients, and I could talk to you forever about writing. Thank you for trusting me with your words, your fears, and your hopes. Ann K., especially, you've been with me through my evolution as an editor and writing coach. And Tracy B., you constantly encourage and inspire me.

My blog readers, your comments are why I keep writing. My accountability partner, David W., your encouragement ("no slumps!") always came at just the right moment. Kris Emery and Cory Emberson, your professional editing, formatting, and proofreading skills are unmatched.

There are a few people who have influenced my life and may never know it, but most especially it was Michael Hyatt's book, *Platform: Getting Noticed in a Noisy World,* that completely changed and opened up what I thought was possible in this life.

And, of course, my life would be nothing without the love of Christ.

About the Author

*"Life is an adventure,
and this is only the beginning."*

MORGAN GIST MACDONALD is a writing coach and editor of nonfiction writing, as well as the founder of Paper Raven Books. She lives in Houston, Texas, with her husband and three children—Cora, Ewan, and Meredith.

When Morgan is not writing or talking about writing, she enjoys reading anything from history to sci-fi/fantasy, playing nerdy Euro board games, and occasionally picking up a tennis racket. Morgan and her family also love to travel.

APPENDIX A

Resources to help your book-writing journey

The craft of writing

Books

Goins, Jeff. *You are a Writer (so start acting like one)*

King, Stephen. *On Writing: A Memoir Of The Craft*

Zinsser, William. *On Writing Well*

Strunk, William and E.B. White. *The Elements of Style, Fourth Edition*

Hyatt, Michael. *Writing a Winning Non-Fiction Book Proposal* http://michaelhyatt.com/writing-a-winning-book-proposal

Blogs

Paper Raven Editing (of course!)
http://www.paperravenediting.com/

Kris Emery,
http://krisemery.com/

Goins, Jeff,
http://goinswriter.com/

The Write Life,
http://thewritelife.com/

The Writing Whisperer,
http://www.thewritingwhisperer.com/

Writer's Digest,
http://www.writersdigest.com/

Writing as a business

Books

Hyatt, Michael. *Platform: Get Noticed in a Noisy World*

Platt, Sean and Johnny B.Truant, *Write. Publish. Repeat: The No-Luck-Required Guide to Self-Publishing Success*

Kawasaki, Guy. *APE: Author, Publisher, Entrepreneur—How to Publish a Book*

Bolt, Chandler. *Book Launch: How to Write, Market & Publish Your First Bestseller in Three Months or Less AND Use it to Start and Grow a Six Figure Business*

Grahl, Tim. *Your First 1,000 Copies: The Step-by-Step Guide to Marketing Your Book*

Blogs

The Book Designer,
http://www.thebookdesigner.com/
Copyblogger,
http://www.copyblogger.com/
Men with Pens,
http://menwithpens.ca/
Jane Friedman,
http://janefriedman.com/
The Creative Penn,
http://www.thecreativepenn.com/
Self-Publishing Advice Blog,
http://www.selfpublishingadvice.org/

Podcasts

The Self-Publishing Podcast,
http://selfpublishingpodcast.com/about/
The Creative Penn,
http://www.thecreativepenn.com/podcasts/

Writing as a Lifestyle

Books

Pressfield, Steven. *The War of Art: Break Through Blocks and Win Your Inner Creative Battles*

Pressfield, Steven. *Do The Work: Overcome Resistance and Get Out of Your Own Way*

Pressfield, Steven. *Turning Pro: Tap Your Inner Power and Create Your Life's Work*

APPENDIX B

Tracking your progress

I used a Google Sheet to track my writing progress, so that my accountability partner could keep tabs on me. My original goal was to write my 25,000-word e-book in seven weeks, at a pace of 5,000 words per week. A few weeks in, I changed my goal to finishing in eight weeks.

You'll see from the screenshot of my Google sheet (below) that life happens. My prime writing time is in the morning, before the day starts. I intended to wake up with my newborn for her first feeding and write before the rest of the house woke up. This worked out well approximately 50% of the time. During Week 6, the baby wasn't sleeping well, so my morning routine was nonexistent. During Week 7, she was sleeping too well, and I slept right through my morning writing sessions.

Life happens. Adjust. But keep tracking your progress!

Below is the screenshot of my Google Sheet, completely legit, unedited. And it did take me almost 10 weeks to finish the first draft.

If you get behind, that's okay. Just press on.

Week 1

Date	Day	Time	Minutes	Words	Working on/notes
15-02-16	Monday	6:30-6:50am	20	1,013	free writing
15-02-17	Tuesday	9:00-9:20pm	20	910	free writing
15-02-18	Wednesday	6:40-7:00am	20	912	free writing
15-02-19	Thursday	6:45-7:05am	20	806	free writing
15-02-21	Saturday	8:00-8:55pm	40	1,613	free writing
				5,254	

Weekly Review

word count met?	yes
results?	free writing, rough organization
struggles:	focus
goal for next week:	finished rough organization

Week 2

Date	Day	Time	Minutes	Words	Working on/notes
15-02-23	Monday	6:50-7:05am	15	653	rough outlining
15-02-25	Wednesday	12:15-12:35	20	716	rough outlining
15-02-27	Friday	2:55-3:15pm	20	632	rough outlining
15-02-28	Saturday	4:35-4:55pm	20	752	started writing the first chapter!
15-02-28	Sunday	6:00-6:20am	20	1,056	have a lot of writing to do Sunday...
				3,809	

Weekly Review

word count met?	no, 1,200 short
results?	rough outline, wrote chapter on myths
struggles:	need to find two days when I can do multiple writing sessions
goal for next week:	chapters on why, preventing self-sabotage

Week 3

Date	Day	Time	Minutes	Words	Working on/notes
15-03-02	Monday	6:05-6:20am	15	475	why write a book
15-03-03	Tuesday	9:05-9:25am	20	807	why write a book and preventing self-sabotage
15-03-04	Wednesday	6:30-6:50am	20	814	preventing self-sabotage, resources appendix

Week 1

Date	Day	Time	Minutes	Words	Working on/notes
15-02-16	Monday	6:30-6:50am	20	1,013	free writing
15-02-17	Tuesday	9:00-9:20pm	20	910	free writing
15-02-18	Wednesday	6:40-7:00am	20	912	free writing
15-02-19	Thursday	6:45-7:05am	20	806	free writing
15-02-21	Saturday	8:00-8:55pm	40	1,613	free writing
				5,254	

Weekly Review

word count met?	yes
results?	free writing, rough organization
struggles:	focus
goal for next week:	finished rough organization

Week 2

Date	Day	Time	Minutes	Words	Working on/notes
15-02-23	Monday	6:50-7:05am	15	653	rough outlining
15-02-25	Wednesday	12:15-12:35	20	716	rough outlining
15-02-27	Friday	2:55-3:15pm	20	632	rough outlining
15-02-28	Saturday	4:35-4:55pm	20	752	started writing the first chapter!
15-02-28	Sunday	6:00-6:20am	20	1,056	have a lot of writing to do Sunday...
				3,809	

Weekly Review

word count met?	no, 1,200 short
results?	rough outline, wrote chapter on myths
struggles:	need to find two days when I can do multiple writing sessions
goal for next week:	chapters on why, preventing self-sabotage

Week 3

Date	Day	Time	Minutes	Words	Working on/notes
15-03-02	Monday	6:05-6:20am	15	475	why write a book
15-03-03	Tuesday	9:05-9:25am	20	807	why write a book and preventing self-sabotage
15-03-04	Wednesday	6:30-6:50am	20	814	preventing self-sabotage, resources appendix

Week 1

Date	Day	Time	Minutes	Words	Working on/notes
15-02-16	Monday	6:30-6:50am	20	1,013	free writing
15-02-17	Tuesday	9:00-9:20pm	20	910	free writing
15-02-18	Wednesday	6:40-7:00am	20	912	free writing
15-02-19	Thursday	6:45-7:05am	20	806	free writing
15-02-21	Saturday	8:00-8:55pm	40	1,613	free writing
				5,254	

Weekly Review

word count met?	yes
results?	free writing, rough organization
struggles:	focus
goal for next week:	finished rough organization

Week 2

Date	Day	Time	Minutes	Words	Working on/notes
15-02-23	Monday	6:50-7:05am	15	653	rough outlining
15-02-25	Wednesday	12:15-12:35	20	716	rough outlining
15-02-27	Friday	2:55-3:15pm	20	632	rough outlining
15-02-28	Saturday	4:35-4:55pm	20	752	started writing the first chapter!
15-02-28	Sunday	6:00-6:20am	20	1,056	have a lot of writing to do Sunday...
				3,809	

Weekly Review

word count met?	no, 1,200 short
results?	rough outline, wrote chapter on myths
struggles:	need to find two days when I can do multiple writing sessions
goal for next week:	chapters on why, preventing self-sabotage

Week 3

Date	Day	Time	Minutes	Words	Working on/notes
15-03-02	Monday	6:05-6:20am	15	475	why write a book
15-03-03	Tuesday	9:05-9:25am	20	807	why write a book and preventing self-sabotage
15-03-04	Wednesday	6:30-6:50am	20	814	preventing self-sabotage, resources appendix

Week 1

Date	Day	Time	Minutes	Words	Working on/notes
15-02-16	Monday	6:30-6:50am	20	1,013	free writing
15-02-17	Tuesday	9:00-9:20pm	20	910	free writing
15-02-18	Wednesday	6:40-7:00am	20	912	free writing
15-02-19	Thursday	6:45-7:05am	20	806	free writing
15-02-21	Saturday	8:00-8:55pm	40	1,613	free writing
				5,254	

Weekly Review

word count met?	yes
results?	free writing, rough organization
struggles:	focus
goal for next week:	finished rough organization

Week 2

Date	Day	Time	Minutes	Words	Working on/notes
15-02-23	Monday	6:50-7:05am	15	653	rough outlining
15-02-25	Wednesday	12:15-12:35	20	716	rough outlining
15-02-27	Friday	2:55-3:15pm	20	632	rough outlining
15-02-28	Saturday	4:35-4:55pm	20	752	started writing the first chapter!
15-02-28	Sunday	6:00-6:20am	20	1,056	have a lot of writing to do Sunday...
				3,809	

Weekly Review

word count met?	no, 1,200 short
results?	rough outline, wrote chapter on myths
struggles:	need to find two days when I can do multiple writing sessions
goal for next week:	chapters on why, preventing self-sabotage

Week 3

Date	Day	Time	Minutes	Words	Working on/notes
15-03-02	Monday	6:05-6:20am	15	475	why write a book
15-03-03	Tuesday	9:05-9:25am	20	807	why write a book and preventing self-sabotage
15-03-04	Wednesday	6:30-6:50am	20	814	preventing self-sabotage, resources appendix

APPENDIX C

How to Create a Reverse Outline

You start writing a book with the best of intentions—and hopefully a draft of a rough organization—but when you get in the flow of writing, you start veering off the road map, adding in extra points, elaborating here, trimming something out there. By the time you've written your first draft, the manuscript may look different than your original plan. You may not even realize how much you've sidetracked, but your reader will definitely notice every section of the book that is unclear, tangential, or just doesn't make sense.

You want the book to be easy to follow because the only way a reader will understand your writing, be inspired by your message, and share your book with others is if the reader completely "gets" what you're trying to say.

The best tool to ensure a streamlined, clear book structure is a reverse outline. As a writing coach and editor of nonfiction writing, I use a reverse outline *every single time* I edit a client's writing or my own.

A reverse outline is basically a traditional outline that you create after you've already written the book. It's an outline done in reverse order, at the end of the writing process, instead of the beginning.

After you finish the first draft, go back to page one. You'll do a full read-through of your manuscript, reading quickly and taking notes. You can take notes by hand, with a pen and a notebook or a stack of note cards, or you can open up a document side-by-side, sharing the screen with your manuscript.

Start by writing down the chapter title. Then, as you read each paragraph, create a sub point in the outline that summarizes the paragraph in one sentence or phrase. With every paragraph that you read, write down a sub point underneath the previous one.

> *Important:* you are only looking at the structure of the manuscript here, which means that you're staying at paragraph-level. You're not adjusting individual sentences

> or wording or even spelling. Ignore all of that. If you get sucked into looking at details, you will not be able to maintain a broad overview of the manuscript.

When you're finished, you'll have an outline that accurately reflects the point that each paragraph is making, in the order that the points are presented in the chapter.

Repeat for every chapter. Once you've finished the last page, you'll have a full outline of your entire book, with each paragraph represented by a summary point.

Now, looking at the whole structure of your book, ask yourself:

- Are there any chapters where I repeat material that was presented in another chapter? Would it be better to combine that repeated material? Or should I clarify why I cover similar material in two different places in the manuscript?
- Are the chapters in the best order? Or is there a chapter that should come earlier or later in the manuscript?
- Within each chapter, do I repeat any points?
- Are there any points that are important but not fully explained, that could benefit from additional material?

- Within each chapter, are there any paragraphs where I go off on a tangent?
- Within each chapter, are there paragraphs that I could group together under one heading?

Within each chapter, are there any places where I could help the reader follow my logical flow? For example: "I'd like to talk about three writing habits... The first habit is... The second habit is... The third habit is..." It doesn't have to be formulaic, but it should be easy for the reader to follow.

The reverse outline of your draft gives you a broad view of the main points in your book so that you know exactly where you need to delete, rearrange, and add to those points.

Make notes in the actual reverse outline, itself—maybe with comment bubbles in your Word document, maybe with sticky notes on an actual paper version of the reverse outline, maybe written in a different color on the note cards—whatever works for your system.

With the reverse outline of your first draft in hand, you have a road map for your revisions. You'll feel confident that you're making the right adjustments to the draft because you'll know how the entire manuscript looks now and how you want it to look when you're finished with revisions.

Take a break, preferably for at least a day. When you're refreshed, you'll be ready for the first edit.

The reverse outline will take a few hours, but it is so worth the effort. Your book will be streamlined, logical, and easy to follow because of the work you put into a reverse outline.

Have fun with the process! It's like building with Legos. There's no wrong way to structure a book, but being intentional about the structure is always best.

I usually do my reverse outline with paper and pen. I went ahead and typed up a reverse outline the first few pages of my chapter, titled "Good writing habits." I've included the original text from the first draft, followed by the reverse outline, so you can see how I changed the structure around in the published version.

Hope this helps!

Excerpt from chapter "Good writing habits"

This is an unedited first draft version.

Habits - they seem like the holy grail of life, right? If only I had the habit of running every day, I'd be in shape. If only I had the habit of meditating every day, I would be a calmer, more sane person. If only I had the habit of grocery shopping regularly, I would eat healthier. If only I had the habit of reading every day, I would have more mental focus. If only I had the habit of writing every day, I would actually be able to write a book. So, you try to adopt one new habit (or two or five new habits), but a week or two in, you let it slide, and you just never quite recover.

Let's have a heart-to-heart here. You bought

this book, you've read the first few chapters, you've probably already started to write book (maybe several times). You need more than just interest in writing a book, you need to commit to writing a book.

Look, you don't have to write every day for the rest of your life to be a writer. Productivity comes in seasons and in spurts. There's no way your life can be a perfect balance of writing every day, reading every day, meditating every day, running every day, and cooking 3 meals a day every day. Okay, maybe someone out there who doesn't have a job, kids, spouse, friends, or hobbies can do all those things every day.

You pick something that you want to focus on for this upcoming season of life (whether that's a few months or a few years), and you just go for it.

It's decision time - right here, right now.

Do you want to write a book?

Do you want to commit the next few months of your life to getting this book written, published, and into the hands of the people who need to read it?

If your answer is, "Not right now, but maybe later," put down this book. It's not worth your time. When you're ready, you can always come back to this book.

If your answer is, "Hell, yes!" now we have something to talk about.

Let's talk about how you're going to write your book.

How long to commit to writing a book? It

depends on the length of the book. You could write a shorter 15,000-20,000 word e-book (that's 60-80 pages) in 6 weeks, easily. This sort of quick e-book is great for building your platform, growing your business, getting your message out to the world fast, positioning yourself as an expert in your field. If you're going for a full-length manuscript, that'll probably be more like 50,000-70,000 words (200-280 pages), you should plan for 4 months of writing. This longer book can help establish you as a true authority, someone who really knows her stuff about her field.

You may not have a clue how long you want the book to be yet, and that's okay. Plan for 3 months of writing, and you'll be covered. Can you change your life so that writing is your priority for the next 3 months? If you can, let's talk nitty gritty.

Write on only one or two devices. With different desktops at home and at the office, laptops for travel, phones with Google docs, and tablets with full writing software on them, it's tempting to just write wherever you happen to be with whatever device you happen to have. But it's going to get very confusing, very quickly. There are sometimes compatibility issues with different software, but that's only half the problem.

The other half of the problem with writing on 5-6 devices is that you're probably not in an actual routine. I won't say that you have write in the same place, at the same time every day, but you should have some rhythms around your writing life. Let's lay out the two different scenarios, and you can judge for yourself which is most likely to produce a book.

Scenario 1: You have a pretty fluid schedule, and you try to roll with what the week has to offer. Sometimes you write at your office computer during lunch. Other days you're busy, so you dictate notes to yourself while you drive home. If it was an activity-filled week with the kids, you might put the little ones to bed early and let the older ones watch a movie, while you sneak away with your laptop for a few minutes of writing time. On travel days, you might type out some notes on your tablet while waiting at the terminal. On a very rare productive morning, you decide to set the alarm early, wake up and add notes on your laptop at the kitchen table.

Scenario 2: Your week can be pretty unpredictable, so you have a couple of times when you try to write. First, you aim to write in the morning, before the day gets going. You set an alarm and enjoy a cup of coffee while writing at the kitchen table. But, you're human, and sometimes the morning just doesn't work out. So, you have a back-up plan A - writing at your office desktop during your lunch break. Of course, sometimes a co-worker invites you to lunch or there's a meeting, in which case you have back-up plan B, skipping the TV show before bed and writing for a few minutes on your laptop at home.

Both scenarios assume that you're a busy person. Believe me, I've never worked with an author who wasn't busy. Heck, I don't know that

I've had a conversation with anyone in the last 10 years who didn't profess to be "crazy busy." Still, do you see the difference between Scenario 1 and Scenario 2? Sure, Scenario 1, you may seem like you're squeezing writing time into every corner of your schedule (that's productive, right?) but your writing is bound to be scattered because you are writing in so many places on so many devices. And there are no plans or intentions to try to write at certain times of the day. If you don't set expectations with yourself that you'll write at X time in X location, then you can't say that you didn't meet your goal. There was no goal. So it's easy to let yourself off the hook.

In Scenario 2, you see the benefit of having a primary writing time, with the back-up plans, in case life gets busy. There's an expectation that you'll write in the morning, but if something happens, you'll know to check in with your schedule at lunch time, and if the lunch time writing doesn't happen, check in with yourself again before you turn on the TV at bed time. Pretty straightforward, you'll know at the end of the day whether you met your goal of writing, and you'll know which part of the day didn't work out. Then, you can begin to notice patterns of when writing actually works best for you.

The other aspect of being intentional about when and where you're writing is that context is important for the brain's ability to organize thoughts. [*cite study] There have been studies on college students who are studying for exams. The college students who reviewed their notes in the classroom in which the exam will be taken consistently performed better than the college students who reviewed their notes in a variety of other locations (library, coffee shop, dorm room, etc). Your brain creates neural pathways of association, and your physical environment provides triggers for those associations.

Imagine you're writing in your favorite space in your home. When you look up from your screen or paper to gather your thoughts, your eyes tend to rest on a particular object - maybe your kitchen clock, maybe your yoga mat by the TV, maybe the bushes outside the window. Your eyes are taking in the physical environment while thinking. The objects around you when you're writing are essentially part of the neural pathways of association. So, having rhythms of writing in a few locations on a limited number of devices increases the chances that you'll remember what you wanted to write about. [*I'm not explaining this well. Revisit.]

Some people swear by certain software programs, and the software changes every few years. I will start by saying that the software is not nearly as important as your commitment to write regularly, on whatever your have available. For most of human history, books have been written with pen and paper, if the author was lucky, so it's silly to assume that there's a huge difference between writing a book with Microsoft Word and writing a book with Scrivener or Google Docs.

Let's face it, no matter what the interface is, writing a book still mostly amounts to you typing a heck of a lot of words into your computer.

Chapter: Good writing habits

Habits help you improve in a variety of aspects in life, but if you let commitment slide, you won't improve.

You have to commit to writing habits.

You don't have to practice habit every day in order to see improvement; you don't have to write every day to write a book.

Can you commit to good writing habits in this upcoming season of life?

The length of writing season will depend on the length of your book.

If you don't know how long the book will be, commit 3 months.

[Header: Habit #1: Writing Routines]

[Routine #1] Write on only one or two devices because of compatibility and syncing issues.

[Routine #2] The other problem with trying to write on more than two devices is lack of writing routine.

Scenario 1: Trying to write at sporadic times of the day, whenever you can fit it in, on whatever device is handy.

Scenario 2: Planning your primary writing session ahead of time and having two specific backup plans.

When you're writing sporadically, with no specific goals, it's easy to let writing habits slip and let yourself off the hook.

Having specific writing goals and plans lets you see which writing habits work for you and which don't so you can establish successful habits.

The other benefit of being intentional about when and where you're writing is that familiar environments help create associations in your memory.

Writing in the same place helps trigger memories around what you were writing about.

[Tangent? Delete?]

[Routine #3] Pick one writing software, and stick with it.

APPENDIX D

Feedback Table

Here's a portion of my feedback table for this book. I removed the names of my beta readers, but all the rest is true to form. You could create a table like this in Excel, Google Sheets, Word, or Google Doc.

Reviewer's Input	My Responses	Where in the MS?
More stories and quotes. "I would also consider adding more personal anecdotes – stories from working with clients, quotes from clients, your own writing journey, quotes from famous authors." [Name]	There are several good quotes from Pressfield, Williams, and White.	One before the intro, and several in the beginning chapters – being a successful author and preventing self-sabotage.
More engaging beginning "The beginning section was a little slow for me." [Name] "The beginning didn't flow as smoothly as the coaching section." [Name]	Bring in a more active voice, not preachy, but inspiring, get the reader excited about the possibilities for her book	Chapter on why writing a book
Re-word tech-heavy language "You have some information about software or systems that you use, but for the uneducated, could use some more explaining. I know you're a big Scrivener and Evernote writer, but for those who have never heard of those, a little more explaining about what they are, what they do, where to find them, etc. would be helpful." [Name]	Explain that Evernote is an app, tone down the Scrivener love, be more software inclusive	Chapter on Good writing habits
New title for last chapter "The finishing and shipping section seemed to be mis-labeled. I was expecting a "what to do with my book now that's it's finished" section. You	It's called "Finishing and Shipping" now, but there's nothing about shipping, and I don't want to go	Title of last chapter

New title for last chapter "The finishing and shipping section seemed to be mis-labeled. I was expecting a "what to do with my book now that's it's finished" section. You are clear in that section that at this stage in the process, you are done with the writer. Maybe re-title that chapter or change the content to match the title." [Name]	It's called "Finishing and Shipping" now, but there's nothing about shipping, and I don't want to go into that. Just "Finishing," then.	Title of last chapter
Citations "Footnotes can be tricky and messy in ebooks. I always recommend incorporating the citation into the text if it's important enough. I see you have 12. How attached are you to this method of referencing?" [Name]	I don't think I can note websites and such in parentheses. I'll keep the footnotes, maybe make them endnotes.	Endnotes

Postive comments:

"I think it's a great message, and one that a lot of people could use to make a positive change in their lives. You do a really nice job of laying out a thorough yet easy to follow guide from start to finish. The outline of practical techniques plus the honest confrontation of mindset and internal aspects of writing work together to really give authors the tools and perspective needed to set goals and make them happen." [Name]

"Once I started reading the actual coaching sections, your book flowed and sang." [Name]

Made in the USA
Middletown, DE
17 January 2016